. . . .

CHOOSING HOPE

. . . .

D1566110

· · · · · · · · · · · · · · ·

GINNY DENNEHY

with SHELLEY FRALIC

· · · · · · · · · · · · · · ·

Choosing Hope

· · · · · · · · · · · · · ·

A MOTHER'S STORY
OF LOVE,
LOSS, AND SURVIVAL

· · · · · · · · · · · · · ·

GREYSTONE BOOKS

Vancouver / Berkeley

Greystone Books
www.greystonebooks.com

Cataloguing data available from Library and Archives Canada

ISBN 978-1-77100-034-5 (pbk.)
ISBN 978-1-77100-035-2 (ebook)

Editing by Barbara Pulling
Copyediting by Shirarose Wilensky
Cover and text design by Jessica Sullivan
Printed and bound in Canada by Friesens
Distributed in the U.S. by Publishers Group West

We gratefully acknowledge the financial support of the
Canada Council for the Arts, the British Columbia Arts Council,
the Province of British Columbia through the Book
Publishing Tax Credit, and the Government of Canada through
the Canada Book Fund for our publishing activities.

Greystone Books is committed to reducing the
consumption of old-growth forests in the books it publishes.
This book is one step toward that goal.

. . . .

To my beautiful boy,
Kelty Patrick,
and my dear sweet babes,
Riley Rae

. . . .

Contents

Prologue

I **DIDN'T WANT** to go on the business trip to Florida, but Kelty insisted. "Mom, don't worry, go," he told me. "I will be all right."

But it didn't feel right. It hadn't felt right for months, not since our beautiful seventeen-year-old son had been gripped by a depression so incapacitating that he would curl up in my arms, crying, "Mom, I just want to be normal like everyone else." The disease had made him so hopeless that he would tell his father, "Dad, I don't know what's wrong with me. This thing grabbed me."

And it wouldn't let go.

We all knew he was in trouble: his fifteen-year-old sister, Riley; his father, Kerry; and me. We tackled it head on, taking Kelty to doctors and clergy and counsellors, making sure he took his medication, and ensuring we were always there for him. When Kelty asked his dad to hide his hunting guns, Kerry hid the hunting guns. When Kelty said he didn't think he could go back to school, we knew we'd find another way for him to finish his senior year. The details didn't matter. Only Kelty did.

2 · CHOOSING HOPE

So when my son insisted he didn't want me to miss that conference in February 2001, I went. I wanted him to know that I believed in him, that I wasn't afraid to leave him for a day or two, even though my heart was heavy as I drove away from the house and headed to the airport.

I wanted to believe that Kelty would be fine.

But he wasn't.

The phone message light was flashing in my hotel room in Orlando when I went back there just before dinner. The message was from Kerry, telling me I needed to call him right away. When I reached him, I learned he was at the Whistler medical clinic with Kelty. It's hard to remember exactly what he said. At first he didn't want to tell me the details, worried because I was alone. But I made him. He had found our son, a garden hose wrapped around his neck, hanging from the cedar beam in my loft office, the airy room in our house that overlooks the mountain peaks where Kelty loved to snowboard.

Some friends at the conference helped me through the fog of the next few hours, booking my flight home and making sure I got on the plane. Two days later, on March 2, we took our beautiful boy off life support, and he died with his mom and dad, his sister, and his devoted nanny by his side.

To live without Kelty seemed impossible. The loss was so deep and the pain was so overwhelming that we felt our family would never recover. We didn't know it then, but the searing sorrow that comes when a parent loses a child would be compounded eight years later when we lost our daughter.

This is their story, the story of Kelty and Riley, a chronicle of family love and loss. But also a story about moving forward and making sense of the incomprehensible.

It is a story about choosing hope.

(1)

·················

Family Ties

·················

MY CHILDHOOD MEMORIES are half a century old, dusty snippets of play and parties and flashes of time and place distilled through the filter of youth, which recalls only what really matters: the feeling of being safe and loved within the protective cocoon of family.

But I will never forget the day my dad died.

I was six, my sister Cath was not yet nine, and our little brother and sister, Robbie and Nancy, the twins, were almost three. In the midst of our happy, chaotic life, it was confusing to walk in the back door of our Montreal house on the afternoon of June 13, 1959, and find sombre strangers milling around.

Who were these people? Why was that woman with the pinched face saying over and over to Cath and me: "Oh, you poor little girls, you poor little girls." Why was our mom sitting on the couch crying and holding the twins so tightly? Why was someone telling us that our dad had been killed in a car accident?

It couldn't be real.

Our father, Edward Pointz Wood, whom everyone called E.P., was to us simply our big strong dad. Even though he was away a lot working, when he was home, he was really there, and he loved us and played with us.

So how could our dad be dead? He was our dad. He was invincible.

E.P. wasn't just our hero; he was everyone's hero. Born in Ontario, an only child, he devoted his life to the service of his country, and that didn't change when he married my mom, Barbara Spear. They first laid eyes on each other at the air force base in Winnipeg. Dad was a squadron leader in the Canadian Forces and something of a ladies' man who never missed the base dances in the 17 Wing mess. Mom was twenty-six then, working as a model and doing volunteer work at the local hospital. When she and her girlfriends wanted to go out and have some fun, they'd head to the base to meet handsome servicemen. My parents met there and fell in love.

Mom and Dad were married on December 29, 1949. Mom settled into life as a military wife knowing that although her husband's work was prestigious and would provide security for the family soon to come along, theirs would be a life on the move. They were living in Winnipeg when my big sister Catherine was born in August 1950. I came along two years later—Virginia Joan, born on September 10, 1952. Over the next few years, our little family would pack and unpack in air force bases all over Europe before Mom took us back home to Winnipeg while Dad was taking courses in Toronto. It was there the twins were born in July 1956.

Two years later, we were on the move again, joining Dad in Montreal. The six of us settled into a lovely house in the enclave of Saint-Bruno, right across the street from the home of the daughter of Governor General Georges Vanier. It was an era when kids spent their days roaming their neighbourhoods until the streetlights lit up the dark. We got into all manner of mischief, most of it harmless, like testing our luck and pluck by sticking our tongues to the metal stair railings of the Vanier residence on the coldest days of winter, which invariably sent our friends screaming for Mom. We had to endure her frantic scolding as she flew out of the house with a pot of warm water to unpeel our bleeding, shredded tongues from the freezing metal.

And then, suddenly, Daddy was dead, and everything changed. Even as I grew older and came to understand the vagaries of life, I would always wonder how it made any sense that a brave man who led his pilots through D-Day, who was wounded during the Dieppe raid, who survived ditching his plane in the North Sea and was awarded a Distinguished Flying Cross in 1944 could make it home safely, only to be killed fifteen years later when someone broadsided his vehicle at a traffic intersection.

We didn't go to the funeral. Young children usually weren't included in the ceremonial rites of the day. Despite our bewilderment and grief and confusion about what it all meant now that Dad was gone, we were expected to pull up our socks and get on with things.

It didn't take long before we were once again on the move. Grams Spear, Mabel, came out that summer, packed us up and shepherded us onto the big ship that took us east across the Great Lakes and to the waiting train that would deliver us to our new life in Winnipeg. Mom's support system, all her family and her friends, were there, not just her mother and stepfather but her younger brother, my Uncle Bob, and his wife, Rae.

Rae first met our family when she was a nurse at Winnipeg General Hospital. Mom, Uncle Bob, and Grams were there regularly to visit my grandfather Elmer Spear, who was very sick with liver cancer. Rae and Mom serendipitously met up again in Germany when their husbands were stationed at the same base. They became good friends, and when Rae's husband was killed in Germany in a training accident, she returned to Winnipeg and ended up marrying my Uncle Bob.

As children do, we soon adapted to life without our dad. The five of us settled into a comfortable home at 218 Waterloo in the prosperous River Heights area of Winnipeg, surrounded by other gracious houses lining the boulevards. We were just blocks from the Assiniboine River. I entered Grade 2 at Robert H. Smith Elementary, Cath was in Grade 4, and the twins were still at home. When Mom decided to get a job at Polo Park shopping centre, she hired a nanny and started working at Rene's for Gifts, which wrapped everything in little pink boxes tied with black ribbons. Locals called the store the "widow's den" because all the women who worked there had lost their husbands.

We were lucky; ours was a family of some means, and we did not go without. Grams's dad, our great-grandfather, was William L. Parrish, a Brandon-born entrepreneur who had co-founded a successful grain company in 1909 with a young Ontario businessman named Norman Heimbecker. The firm, Parrish and Heimbecker, became well known for its agri-food products, including the Butterball turkey that has graced many a Thanksgiving dinner table. Over the next century, it would grow into a nationwide company with interests in grain shipping (one hundred grain elevators across Canada) and become the second biggest manufacturer of flour in the country. The company exported peas to Cuba and flour to China. Today, it operates numerous inland grain terminals and employs 1,400 people. When Grams and our grandfather married in 1920, he was not a wealthy man. He had studied architecture and was a captain in the Royal Naval Air Service in the First World War, but after the war he had returned home and bought a gas station with a partner. He moved on to work for a company that sold auto parts, and eventually he bought that business, which he renamed R.E. Spear Limited. It became the largest manufacturers' agent for automotive parts in western Canada. When my grandfather died in 1953, Uncle Bob took over. Two years later, Grams married our new granddad, Cecil Philip, who was a reserved, very proper judge.

Those first years back in Winnipeg seemed to suit us. Cath and I made friends at school and in the neighbourhood, and Mom seemed to be adjusting to life without our father. For a time, things were good.

But it wouldn't last.

In the summer of 1960, the year after our dad died, Mom packed the four of us kids into the car for a road trip to Montreal. She wanted to show us the place where we'd lived and spent time with our father. While we were there, she began feeling an intense pain in her chest, and once we were back home, the news was grim. She was diagnosed with breast cancer and by September had undergone a mastectomy, though no chemotherapy or radiation. While the details of that time are dim, I remember the day Cath and I were sat down and gently told that our mother was sick and that we were being sent away to school and would have to sleep there. Balmoral Hall was a private, girls-only boarding school in Winnipeg, and everyone felt us going there was for the best. As it turned out, I was the youngest boarder the school had ever accepted.

I was an adventurous child, and boarding school sounded like an adventure. Cath, who was more responsible, wasn't so sure. The twins were too young to really know what was going on, and they were to stay home with a nanny looking after them while Mom battled her illness.

At Balmoral Hall, Cath and I were put up in bunk beds in the residence called the White House. We were able to stay together, which made it easier. We weren't just sisters, we were best friends, and to be near each other meant everything. Cath missed her friends from public school, but I felt like I belonged in this new place. The staff were always around ensuring we were doing our work and behaving, and that seemed to give me comfort.

Balmoral Hall, though a non-religious institution, was as strict as any Catholic girls' school might be, regimented and purposeful about protocol. The headmistress wore a black cloak, and we had to line up regularly for tunic inspection. But the education was a good one: we took Latin and French and music lessons, and the expectation was that we would excel. Cath was a very good student. I fell short on the academic front, a reality somewhat softened when I began to share my Grade 5 locker with Clare Powell, a day student at Balmoral. Clare was dark-haired and pretty, and we shared a sense of mischief that bonded us immediately. She was smart, too, and liked sports and horseback riding. We would become lifelong friends.

Cath and I usually went home on weekends, but it was a sad time. If our mother wasn't in the hospital, she was in her wheelchair, which meant our Saturdays and Sundays were spent quietly. We didn't really understand what was going on; we just wanted her to get better. She was such a beautiful, stoic woman, and if she was in pain or had her dark moments, she never let on.

But as the months went by, her health deteriorated to the point that she was forced into the hospital. She seemed to know she was going to die. One day she sent for Cath and me, and we were each given a few minutes alone with her. Not realizing that we were there to say goodbye, I sat on the edge of her bed and asked her when she was coming home. She gave me a big hug and said, "Snookums, I worry about you more than anyone." Mom knew intuitively that this spirited nine-year-old child of hers, this girl with the tough-on-the-outside bravado—I would try anything and had even learned to ski on a local river bank at the age of three—was already putting up walls to fend off the pain life would throw her way.

A few days after that visit, on a Friday afternoon, Cath and I were at Balmoral Hall waiting for the taxis that would take us, along with our schoolmates, to our regular outing at the Winnipeg Winter Club. It was a break we looked forward to every week, an early evening of swimming lessons, badminton games, and as many French fries as we could eat. But on this afternoon, one of the teachers took Cath and me aside. We wouldn't be able to join our school friends; Uncle Bob and Auntie Rae were coming to pick us up instead. When they arrived, Cath and I noisily piled into their station wagon. Auntie Rae turned to us, sitting in the back of the car, and said, "I have to tell you girls that your mother has died."

Cath burst into tears, a complete waterworks. I sat still and said to myself, over and over, as if that would somehow make it so: "No, she hasn't. No, she hasn't." I didn't make the connection, didn't want to believe it. It couldn't be happening again.

It was February 9, 1962.

We were orphans.

Except, of course, we weren't. My mom had taken much care to ensure that we would be looked after. In the weeks before her death, she had made arrangements with Uncle Bob and Auntie Rae to adopt us, and they had readily agreed.

Mom had been worried, though, that her brother's house wasn't roomy enough. My aunt and uncle had married in 1956—Cath and I were flower girls at their wedding—and when they realized they couldn't have children of their own, they had adopted Robbie, who was born in 1959, and Cheryl, born in 1960. With us in the mix, they were about to become the parents of six children, so a few days before she died, my mom had pulled out a newspaper advertisement and showed her brother a house for sale that she thought would be perfect, one block down from our house on Waterloo. She had no idea that her brother, mindful that the Spear brood would soon include the Wood children, had bought the same house earlier that day.

When my aunt and uncle picked us up from Balmoral that day, they took us for a little drive around the neighbourhood, stopping out front of what would be our new home. It had a long curving driveway and a grand façade, and there was something stately about it that seemed to put me at ease. I already knew this rambling house at 66 Waterloo because I had ridden my bike around its driveway many times.

We moved in a month later, and I loved it. Inside the front door was a huge double staircase, and the main floor had a fancy drawing room and a massive living room with an attached sun porch. The big dining room with its wainscoting and glorious woodwork was toward the back of the house, along with the kitchen. The floors were polished wood, and there were stained-glass windows everywhere. Up the first flight of stairs, on the landing, was a billiards room. Farther along the upper hall were four spacious bedrooms, each with its own sink, and a main bathroom. The two boys shared a bedroom, Nancy and Cheryl each had their own rooms, and my aunt and uncle took the fourth bedroom.

The third floor was magic because that's where Cath and I had our bedrooms and our own bathroom with rose-petal taps. There was another room on our floor, which we called the maid's room. Over the years we sometimes shared our space with a live-in student or a domestic worker who had been hired to help around the house.

The finished basement had a recreation area and a mud room, and the front and back yards were perfect for a bunch of gamboling kids. In fall, we spent hours building forts in the leaves that fell from the oak trees lining the street. Out back, we would flood the yard in winter to create a skating rink.

It was the perfect house for a gaggle of growing kids, and as we had so many times before, my sisters and brother and I settled in quickly. We started calling our aunt and uncle "Mom" and "Dad." Because there were now two Robbies in the household, my brother became Ted in honour of our father, Edward. We didn't talk much among ourselves or with the adults about losing our dad and then our mom. Nobody ever sat us down and tried to explain what it all meant. That was reflective of a time when kids were meant to be seen and not heard and when talking about such things was thought only to make them harder, especially for children.

Even though I loved the new house and there was no hardship or lack of love in our lives, there was a part of me that felt like I didn't belong in this new family. I was the misfit, the one in the middle. I even ran away from home a few times, though my mom and dad were smart enough to start channelling that energy into sports. Much of my spare time was spent at the local winter club, pursuing activities like speed swimming, squash, rowing, badminton, and skating. Cath liked sports, too, but she was far more interested in other diversions, like boys and listening to the Beatles and appearing on *Teen Dance Party* at a local television station.

When Dad wasn't away on business, he was a devoted Shriner, working in the local community. Mom's time was spent raising us kids. Her spare hours were devoted to volunteer work with the junior league and the heart foundation and to her lively social life. She and Dad liked to party and were religious adherents to the daily 5 PM cocktail hour. The house was always filled with family and friends, with kids and noise and food, a steady stream of people coming in and out, whether they were neighbour children running wild around the yard or their parents toasting one another in the drawing room. Although Mom was affectionate, she clearly had her hands full. And a handful we were. Sometimes, when Mom and Dad were away, we were looked after by Betty Stefaniuk. Betty was a bit older than we were, with kids of her own, and she had worked for Grams since the age of sixteen. Betty did her best to stickhandle us, but when Cath and I threw wild parties at our house and the kids started lining up outside trying to get in, Betty would call one of Dad's friends to come over for backup. I was usually the instigator, so when it came time for the lectures, I was always on the receiving end.

I stayed at Balmoral Hall through Grade 6, leaving in Grade 7 to attend River Heights, a public school I hated. I was a fat, dumpy kid, and even though I had friends, they were cute and seemed to have it together. They had boyfriends, and I didn't. I was a fish out of water. I went back to Balmoral Hall for Grade 8.

Cath always did well at her studies, and she was popular, a real social butterfly who was never without a boyfriend. I was a terrible student, so much so that I was politely asked to leave Balmoral Hall after Grade 8 and ended up at Convent of the Sacred Heart. I wouldn't last there, either, after my friends and I were caught smoking. Trying to avoid the cold outside, we had sneaked into the locker rooms, which turned out to be ventilated to the whole school. That did not amuse the five nuns who smelled smoke and opened the door to find us puffing away. It didn't help that we had been caught another time playing catch with the plastic sponges used to sop up the holy water in the chapel. Mother Leonard phoned my dad and asked him to retrieve me, suggesting that Sacred Heart "wasn't the right school for Virginia."

I didn't fare much better at Kelvin High School, acting out and caring far more about my friends and partying than I did about hitting the books. I was a rebel, and so was Clare, who by now was going to nearby Tuxedo Park Secondary. One day as I was heading to the home of a friend after deciding to play hooky, trailing my somewhat reluctant sister Cath and carrying a case of beer we had lifted from our mother, Mom drove by and caught us in the act. She was furious.

I couldn't stop thinking of my real mom. At Christmas I was always convinced that she was going to walk through the front door, that she had just gone away for a while and was surely going to come back. I guess it was what I had to tell myself to survive. When I was twenty, I asked Dad, "Is my mom really dead?" He was shocked. When I pointed out that I didn't even know where she was buried, he drove me over to the cemetery in the fog and showed me her gravestone: "In loving memory of Barbara J. Wood, died Feb. 9, 1962, age 38 years." I finally got to say goodbye to my mom.

If I had a saviour during those wild teen years, it was Grams, with whom I had a special bond. She was tiny, full of warmth and earthy spirit. She was my guardian angel on Earth. And despite my struggles with fitting in, it was a good life, full of all the promise and adventure a teenager could imagine. You just never knew what was going to happen in that big house on Waterloo.

Once, my grandfather won a pig in a contest and decided to give it to my dad. We kids called it Matilda, and the pig moved into the basement mud room. Robbie would walk Matilda up and down Waterloo to exercise her. When the pig got bigger, my dad decided she had to be housed in the garage. Finally, Dad decided that Matilda had outgrown the city and needed to go to our summer house, a spacious family farm on the Red River about thirty kilometres outside of Winnipeg. The property straddled the highway, with the three-thousand-acre Parrish dairy farm on one side and the twenty-six acres surrounding Linton Lodge, named after William Linton Parrish, on the other. The lodge was a sprawling log cabin where we spent most summers. When Dad chose me to transplant Matilda, I dutifully put newspapers down in the back of my red Volkswagen and stuffed in the unhappy porker, who kept jumping between the front and back seats. Once there, I convinced the farm manager to take Matilda off my hands. Not long afterward, we were having our big Easter dinner when my dad, finished with his plate, pushed himself away from the table and said: "Well, how did you like Matilda?"

Summers at the cabin were heaven. It was a cavernous four-bedroom house with numerous outbuildings, including a bunkhouse and a guest cabin, along with a vegetable garden and an in-ground swimming pool we called "the cement pond." There were horses to ride, canoes to paddle, and a boat that my dad would fill with us kids to cruise up and down the river. With Dad you never knew what was coming next: we might arrive at the cabin to find a Shriners' motorcycle club using the property or a clutch of Arabian-style tents set up for the next big lawn party. Dad was funny and generous, the kind of man people were instantly attracted to. If we had to choose someone to raise us, we couldn't have chosen better.

Even though my school years had been tumultuous, I managed to graduate from a special Grades 11/12 collegiate program offered by the University of Winnipeg. Happy to be done with academics, I headed into the work force, taking a teller's job at the Canadian Imperial Bank of Commerce. By then, my life had also taken another important turn.

THAT I WOULD fall in love with Kerry Dennehy seemed inevitable. He was handsome and fun, and his sister Darcy was a friend of Cath's. Being my older sister, Cath always had her radar tuned for dating possibilities for me. After all we had been through, nobody knew me better than she did, and nobody more devotedly had my best interests at heart.

In the summer of 1969, Cath got a job at the Bending Lake Fishing Lodge in northern Ontario, where she began dating a boy named Billy. Kerry was Billy's best buddy, and Cath knew the minute she met him that he was the one for me.

Back home in Winnipeg, she told me: "Oh, Ginny, I found the perfect guy for you." I was seventeen and in Grade 11. I had never had a boyfriend. I was still chubby and rebellious; I had guys for friends, but mostly I just hung out with the crowd. Dating wasn't that important to me, so it took some convincing. But Cath worked on me, said Kerry was a great guy, that he was smart and hard working, and his family lived only a few blocks away from us. She insisted I meet him, and when I finally agreed, she arranged for the four of us to get together at the cabin.

Cath and I were having a quick swim at the cabin when Billy and Kerry pulled into the driveway in Kerry's Jeep. That meant the first sight my future husband would have of me was me hauling my ungainly self out of the pool while wearing a two-piece bathing suit.

We hit it off instantly. He was so tall and good-looking. Cath was right: we talked and laughed and just seemed to click.

Kerry and I started dating, going to parties and to the movies. When I met his family, with his four brothers and one sister, I was in awe. The Dennehys weren't rich, but they were respected. The kids were cool, and I was proud to be part of the mix. They seemed to like me, too. Kerry was kind, and I felt safe with him and his family. I spent as much time at their house as I could.

I was working full time at the bank by then, and Kerry was working for Richardson Securities, as a trader, in the same building. We saw each other every day. I couldn't have been happier, but I also liked to keep Kerry guessing. One of the Winnipeg Blue Bombers who came into the bank kept asking me out on a date, so to tease Kerry I would say, "Kerry, do you think I should go out with him?" But I didn't mean it. The truth was Kerry and I were attached at the hip.

Then a friend convinced me to go on a ski vacation to Banff with her for a week. I fell in love with the place and its freewheeling ski-bum culture, and when I got back to Winnipeg, I told Kerry I was quitting my job and moving. He was hurt and confused. He didn't understand what was going on, and I'm not sure I did either. But two weeks later I was back in Banff, living in a room at the YWCA with no job and no Kerry.

It was an impulsive adventure, and that's all I could see. I was skiing every day and having wild experiences with a like-minded group of amazing young people. I had only been there about a week when the glow began to dim. I phoned home and talked to my mom, hoping she would hear the catch in my voice and ask me to come to my senses and head back to Winnipeg. But she didn't. I stayed there for nearly three years, working as a cocktail waitress in a local bar and as the first female lift operator at Sunshine Village, about forty minutes out of Banff. One of the houses that I rented in town with a dozen or more friends was so crowded that one of my roomies—Leaping Larry, who ran the Wawa T-bar lift—slept in the bathtub.

I dated a bit when I was in Banff and at one point lived in a garage with a boyfriend. But I couldn't stop thinking about Kerry, who had quit his job and moved to Calgary, where he was working as a supervisor in a juvenile detention centre. I knew that I had broken his heart, but we stayed in touch. We had an on-again, off-again relationship for the next few years, seeing each other in Winnipeg on special occasions and writing letters back and forth.

And then one day I had finally gotten Banff out of my system. I turned down a job offer in the Bugaboos and decided that it was time to make something of myself. I applied to the University of British Columbia nursing school in 1973, though I didn't really know what I wanted to do or where I wanted to be. I liked helping people, and Kerry's mother had always said I would make a great nurse. It wasn't that hard to get into university in those days, and I had done a bit of night school to upgrade my marks, so nursing it was.

In Vancouver I shared an apartment with Cath's friend Sharon, who was doing an internship as a dietitian. My parents were paying for my tuition, so I didn't have any money worries. I was soon "rushed" by a sorority and became a Gamma Phi Beta, which was great for my social life in a city of strangers. But I hated nursing. I wasn't cut out for a life as Florence Nightingale. When I fainted during a circumcision demonstration at St. Paul's Hospital, I realized it wasn't the career for me. I decided to go into physical education for my second year, majoring in physiology and minoring in nutrition. It helped that I had been something of a jock. I assisted the professors with fitness testing and eventually became director of the women's intramural program. To earn extra spending money, I taught fitness classes and worked at the Keg. I had four or five jobs during my time at university and needed a car to get to them, so my dad came and bought me a new orange 1973 Beetle. When the salesman asked if it needed a radio, my dad said: "She needs a radio more than she needs the engine."

Kerry was still living in the Prairies, working as a salesman for a company called Atco Structures. He and I continued to date other people, but we still got together occasionally. It was as if we couldn't be together yet didn't know how to be apart. At one point, Kerry was engaged to a law student—he had contemplated becoming a lawyer himself. I fell in love with another man for a brief time, though my relationships never seemed to go anywhere.

Cath had married Billy in 1971, and when that didn't work out, she joined Sharon and me in the apartment in Vancouver, enrolling at UBC and working toward a degree in theatre. But when I graduated in 1978 with a bachelor's degree in physical education, I wasn't sure what to do, so I returned to my roots: I went home, rented an apartment near downtown Winnipeg, and got a job as a fitness trainer at a physical rehabilitation centre. All my friends, including Clare, had married right out of school and were having children, and here I was in my late twenties and unattached. By then Kerry was living in Edmonton. I'd heard through the grapevine that he was getting serious about someone else, and something clicked. I called him and said I wanted to be with him. In what seemed like a heartbeat, I had moved to Edmonton and into Kerry's townhouse, and we were together again. I sold running shoes at Eaton's before landing a position in guest services at the Four Seasons Hotel.

Kerry maintains to this day that I proposed to him, but the truth is I don't remember. I just know that a year later, on June 21, 1980, Kerry and I exchanged vows in front of our family and friends at the cabin on the Red River where we had first met. He was truly the love of my life, and I didn't want to spend another day without him.

(2)

·················

Growing
Up Dennehy

·················

KERRY AND I WERE thrilled to be starting our life together
as newlyweds. We laughed about how long it had taken
us to get there, but now all that mattered was the future
ahead of us. We knew it would be wonderful, that we would
have the family we had always wanted. No matter what, we
would be happy and grow old together.

Kerry was still working for Atco in Edmonton, carv-
ing out a successful career selling construction trailers. I
enjoyed working on the front desk at the Four Seasons.
There's something about the hospitality industry that
appeals to me. Most people look forward to staying in
hotels, whether it's for vacation or business. There's a cer-
tain freedom in locking that hotel room door behind you
and heading out for an adventure in a different city. I've
always thought that's why there's such an air of exuberance
and even mystery in the bustle of a hotel lobby.

Both of us settled into our new routines quickly, and
things were going great. And then we started to get itchy

feet. I had fallen in love with Vancouver while going to UBC and Kerry was equally enamored with the city. The West Coast beckoned.

Kerry asked his Atco bosses for a transfer to their Vancouver operation, and they readily obliged. I talked one of my former UBC professors into giving me a contract job conducting fitness testing around the province, something I had done during my university years. I was good at it, and it was an easy transition for them. So just like that, we were on our way.

Vancouver house prices have always been among the highest in the country, and in the early 1980s mortgage rates were spiking. But we were determined to live in the city. My mother had left me some Parrish and Heimbecker company shares when she died, and I knew that selling a few would give us the financial kick-start we needed. Some of my relatives felt I was selling off the family assets, the legacy left by my great-grandfather William Parrish. But it made sense to me. Wasn't that what money was for? Wasn't that why the shares had been left to me, to help me on my life's path? My popularity in the family didn't improve when my decision caused a small domino effect, prompting other family members, like my sister Cath, to sell some of their shares, too.

Kerry and I used the money for a down payment on a charming little three-bedroom house on Yew Street in Kitsilano, a neighbourhood that in the post-hippie era was still a counterculture haven. The house, one of the original buildings on the old Molson's brewery site, was listed at $145,000. It wasn't much to look at, but the location was great, and it felt like home. We knew we could do something with it, so we kept a bit of the money aside for renovations.

My dad, who had come out from Winnipeg to help us in the house hunt, couldn't believe we were handing over nearly $150,000 for a nondescript house on a postage-stamp-sized city lot. In Winnipeg, that kind of money would buy you a mini-mansion with a big yard. But we loved it. We redid the kitchen, installed skylights to brighten up the small dark rooms, and updated everything that our budget allowed. It was a big job, and it ate up months of our time and much of our energy. Looking back, it was crazy to think we had gotten married, moved to another city, bought a house, and started taking down walls all within a year.

As it turned out, the year would be a rough one for another reason. My beloved Grams had not been well, and when I got a call from my mother in February 1981 telling me that Grams had died, I was overwhelmed. Mom and the rest of the family assured me that because I had just been back to Winnipeg to see her, I didn't really need to go back for Grams's funeral. The decision haunts me to this day. In a way, I never really got to say a proper goodbye or to express my gratitude and love for Grams, one of the most important people in my life.

And then Kerry threw another wrench into the works.

Just before we moved to Vancouver, he and some Edmonton friends had started a little real estate company, Concept III Realty. His friends wanted him to go back and help out with the new business, and he thought that was a good idea. I didn't question it, but I was worried about our finances while he was involved with a fledgling start-up. If we were moving back to Edmonton, I needed to find a real job, with a good salary, benefits, and the promise of future advancement. The only companies I could think of that offered that kind of security were Xerox and IBM. I didn't have any business or technological experience, but I did a little research on both companies, contacted their human resources departments and, amazingly, landed interviews with both firms. Both ended up offering me a job. I chose IBM because when they flew me to Edmonton for a second interview, I immediately connected with the branch manager, Bill Cranston. He was a wonderful man, and I knew I could learn a lot working for him. It was one of the best calls I have ever made.

Not wanting to sell our just-renovated Yew Street home, we decided to rent it out. That gave us enough financial leeway to buy a house in Alberta. Barely a year after leaving, we were back in Edmonton, living in the Sherwood Park area. I started work for IBM as a district purchase specialist, travelling around western Canada and convincing customers to buy the office products they had been renting. I was good at it, and I loved the travel, the people I met, the learning curve I was on, and, of course, the income.

Unfortunately, Concept III Realty didn't turn out as Kerry and his partners had hoped. So, within a year, we made the choice to move back to Vancouver. I loved my job, but Edmonton didn't suit me, never had. IBM was wonderful, not blinking when I asked for a transfer. Kerry hit the job market, doing a number of different things until he passed the Canadian Securities Course and began working as a broker. We settled into a comfortable new routine of work and married life, picking up with old friends and making new ones. We hiked and swam and played tennis and squash and took up that most Vancouver of athletic pursuits: jogging.

In the spring of 1983, I popped into our family doctor's office because I hadn't been feeling that great. I thought I had the flu, so I was completely taken aback when he did an exam and then looked at me and said: "Ginny, you're pregnant."

I couldn't believe it. Kerry and I had talked about having kids, and coming from big families ourselves, we wanted to have a big family of our own. Although we hadn't planned when that might happen, we didn't take precautions after we got married, so my pregnancy shouldn't have been such a surprise. But it was. Kerry was beyond thrilled, as was I. We were having a baby, and life could not have been more perfect.

Baby Dennehy was due October 28. Luckily for me, the pregnancy was uneventful. I didn't have morning sickness and didn't gain much weight. I kept working and even managed to take my daily dip at nearby Kitsilano Pool over the summer. I did stop playing squash for a bit, and I thought better of jogging, which meant I had to forfeit doing the hard 26 miles of another marathon. Kerry and I had first done one before we were married and another in Seattle right afterward. As expectant parents, we did all the exciting firsts: attending prenatal classes, undergoing an ultrasound, prepping Daddy for what he might expect in the delivery room.

A week before the baby was due, I went on maternity leave. Of course, as is so often the case, the baby had other plans, and October 28 came and went. I kept busy, baking furiously and fretting over the nursery. The baby's room was near ours on the second floor. I painted the walls pale green and stocked up on diapers and cozy little green sleepers and blankets for the crib. Everything had a baby animal motif.

I went into labour in the middle of the night. I quietly got out of bed and walked around the house, and when the pain became unbearable, I woke up Kerry and told him it was time to go. He sat up, reached into the bedside table, and pulled out the to-do list from the prenatal class, which for some reason suggested we pack a lunch before leaving for the hospital. So instead of helping me get ready, Kerry did just that: he went right to the kitchen and began making sandwiches and packing cookies. It was hilarious, though less so at the time.

I was in labour for forty-eight hours, two long days hooked up to a fetal monitor. None of the medical tricks worked, and the doctor told us I would probably need to deliver by Caesarean section. I wasn't happy about it, and the baby didn't much like that option either: I suddenly needed to push, and before we knew it, Kelty Patrick was born the old-fashioned way. It was November 23, 1983. In my arms was the most beautiful eight-pound, two-ounce blue-eyed baby boy we had ever seen.

Kerry and I had talked about a name before the baby was born, and both of us liked Kelty. We had a friend in Edmonton named Bruce Kelty, and Kerry's mom, Dodie, had given all of her kids good Irish names. Kerry's dad was Gerald Patrick, so when our baby turned out to be a boy, that middle name seemed to fit. It's hard to explain, but this new little man even looked like a Kelty, robust and raring to get on with life. In his naming, there was also a prescience we could never have imagined—years later, we found out that Kelty roughly translates to "troubled waters."

Kelty was a fussy baby. His lack of interest in breastfeeding was a bit disheartening, and trying to get him to nurse became a chore. Thankfully, my mom came to help out for the first few weeks, and she was a godsend. Kelty eventually took to the bottle, though he wasn't keen about sticking to the schedule Mom and I tried to keep him on. Our new son ruled the roost, which meant he didn't sleep much. And neither did we.

Less than three months after Kelty was born, my boss at IBM convinced me to come back to work. It was a dilemma: I wanted to stay home with Kelty, but we also needed to pay the bills. The feminist revolution that so defined our generation had somehow convinced women that not only could we have it all—marriage, kids, and the career—but that we owed it to our gender to do it all well and without complaint.

The only way it would work for us was to find a nanny. After interviewing, we hired a woman named Sham, who was from Guyana. Sham was wonderful with Kelty, and they took to each other right away. That was very important to me. Kerry had a new job as a general manager for the Earl's restaurant chain, and I was away a lot—IBM decided a group of us needed sales training, which found me in Atlanta a few times during Kelty's first year—so the stability Sham provided made all the difference for us as first-time parents.

I still cooked dinner as often as I could and made homemade baby food, freezing puréed fruit and vegetables in ice cube trays. I loved being a mom and was always buying Kelty new toys and baby clothes, going overboard every time I walked into a store. As any parent can attest, a newborn brings a different level of hectic to a household. We never seemed to get any sleep, and, tough as it is to admit, I used to line up bottles of milk in Kelty's crib so that when he woke up he could grab a bottle, fill his tummy, and fall right back to sleep. I worried that he would become more attached to Sham than to me, and one time, when Kerry brought him to the airport after I returned from a business trip, Kelty played shy with me. It didn't last, but it hurt me to the core to think my baby boy saw me even fleetingly as a stranger.

The Dennehys were Catholics with deep religious roots, and Kerry felt strongly about raising our children as Catholics. As a Protestant, I had no problem with that, but I did tell Kerry that he would need to take responsibility for our son's religious education. He agreed, and Kelty was christened in a little church down the street from us.

Kelty was a restless baby, so it was no surprise that he was walking at nine months, tearing around the house and keeping us on our toes. He was always laughing and making us laugh. He was occasionally plagued by eczema, which meant slathering him with calamine lotion and giving him oatmeal baths, but he took it all in stride. Our boy loved to eat—anything and everything. Most kids would turn up their noses at delicacies like paté, but not Kelty—put it in front of him and it would be gone in a heartbeat. He was happy-go-lucky, full-speed ahead. Chasing ducks at the park or playing down the street with the neighbourhood kids was pretty much the perfect day for him. We spoiled him, of course. His favourite toy was Todeye, a stuffed white bear that he took everywhere. No one can remember where Todeye's name came from, but Kelty seldom let him out of his sight, not caring a whit that all those washings and all that manhandling were starting to wear on the little bear. Every summer, a group of us would head over to a resort on Vancouver Island, and one year we left Todeye behind by mistake. Kelty refused to go to bed without his best friend, so I had to phone the resort and get Todeye sent home immediately by courier.

Kelty couldn't sit still, and the minute he found his feet, he'd started climbing out of his crib. Once, in the middle of the night, I heard a weird "meow" sound, like a distressed kitten, and jumped out of bed to find out what it was. I followed the sound downstairs but couldn't see anything until I opened the door to the basement and saw Kelty, hanging by his tiny fingertips from the back of the open staircase. I fetched the little monkey and put him back to bed, not knowing whether to laugh or cry.

Kerry and I still spent our summers in Winnipeg, splitting our vacation time between my family's cabin and Kerry's family place at Victoria Beach on Lake Winnipeg. When Kelty was about eight months old, we decided to enter him in the annual Victoria Beach summer masquerade parade. We weren't quite sure how to dress him up, but we finally put a big Pampers diaper box over his baby carriage and dubbed it the Pope mobile.

Life was good. We had our families in Manitoba and a big circle of friends in Vancouver, getting together with our kids at each other's homes or nearby parks. We were always going out to dinner parties, the kind where everybody dressed up in crazy costumes. Once Kerry and I showed up in lederhosen for German night, and another time I covered myself with pink balloons for a pink-themed party.

Kerry's job at Earl's was going well. The perks included trips for the managers, usually to exotic places where much dining and drinking was on the menu, and every once in a while I would go along, leaving Kelty in the care of Sham. One junket in late 1985 found Kerry and me travelling all over Europe by train with a group of other Earl's managers and their spouses, visiting vineyards and wineries. I love my wine, and it was a glorious trip, but for some reason, I couldn't drink. We'd get up every morning and go down for a lovely breakfast with Kerry's colleagues, but I couldn't eat, either. All I wanted was a cold glass of milk, which I couldn't find anywhere. I didn't think much of it, figuring I had a touch of the flu.

Kerry had been to the doctor before our trip after discovering an odd bulge on the left side of his abdomen. It didn't hurt, and while they tried to figure out what it was, the doctor told Kerry it was okay to take the trip as long as he avoided contact sports. One night in Barcelona, we were walking back to our hotel after a lovely dinner when we were mugged. Kerry was carrying the bag with all our money and our passports. The mugger knocked me over, then knocked Kerry down and took off with the bag. Kerry set off in hot pursuit. I yelled at him to stop; all I could think of was that he was going to tackle the mugger and hurt himself. Thankfully, he let the guy get away. It was a hassle replacing our papers at the Canadian embassy, but I was just grateful that Kerry was okay. When we returned home, we got the results of his tests. The bulge was a sac full of waste material that his kidney wasn't processing, and Kerry ended up in hospital having the kidney removed. It was a serious operation, and it was difficult afterward to see him laid up and taking drugs for the pain. Thankfully, his physical health and die-hard athleticism stood him in good stead—he recovered well and adjusted to managing with just one kidney.

I had booked my own doctor's appointment after we returned from Europe, and for me the news was better: I was pregnant. We couldn't have been more excited at the thought of welcoming another Dennehy to the family. Our second baby was due in late June 1986, which meant a gap of almost three years between the two. Kelty was just the right age to welcome a new little brother or sister.

My wider family was expanding, too. My sister Cath had been living in Vancouver with her second husband, Rick, and their boys, Rory and Jesse, were born in 1978 and 1980. Their daughter, Tegan, arrived in 1985, after Cath's family moved back to Winnipeg. My sister Nancy had married Ray in 1983; they moved to Scotland, where they adopted two children, Tina and Matthew. My brother Ted married Dyan in 1982 and settled in Vancouver. They had three children: Kailey, Sam, and Lauren. My sister Cheryl married David in 1990. My brother Robbie married Cathy in 1986, and their two children were named Jacqueline and Robbie. Both Robbie and Cheryl still lived in Winnipeg.

It was another good pregnancy. I wasn't sick, and I managed to keep working and doing everything I had been doing before. But at some point, Kerry and I looked around our Yew Street house and knew that with another little one coming, we were outgrowing the place. We also knew we could no longer afford anything on Vancouver's west side. We decided that the North Shore might be the answer, and one day we checked out a rambling modern house on Hadden Drive in the British Properties. I loved it from the moment we walked through the front door. It was a post and beam bungalow in the woods with a walkout basement. A little trail went down to the creek in the ravine out back. It reminded me so much of the family cabin back in Winnipeg—all glass walls, beamed ceilings, and sprawling layout. The house was over our budget, but we bought it anyway.

Our moving date was June 30. Riley was due June 28, which meant I was going to be either very pregnant or packing a newborn during the move. If that wasn't stressful enough, Kerry decided that to save money we would rent a truck rather than hiring movers. On moving day, I was feeling almost as big as our new house, sitting in the front seat of the Budget Rent-a-Truck cradling Kerry's stuffed grayling fish, his prize possession, and wondering what we were thinking. But we got there and managed to unload the truck without me going into labour.

In the midst of the chaos, we'd also had to hire a new nanny because Sham didn't want to move to the North Shore. We interviewed again and ended up taking on Jo, a young woman from England. She told us she wouldn't be able to stay for more than a year or so, but she was the kind of nanny we were looking for, warm and no-nonsense, so we agreed and she moved in with us.

On July 2, with the house full of unpacked boxes, I went into labour in the middle of the night. This time we got up and headed straight to the hospital. The whole way I was in tears, my hormones raging. All I could think about was how different our lives were going to be, how our perfect little family of three was going to change. I was excited, but I was also worried about how it was going to work out. The labour was a tough eighteen hours. But when Riley Rae, our gorgeous baby girl, was born with blue eyes just like her brother's, healthy and hale at eight pounds, eleven ounces, it didn't matter anymore. Kerry and I had already decided on a name. My good friend Susan Dowler's middle name was Riley, and I'd always liked it. Rae was after my mother, Barbara Rae. When we got Kerry's mom, Dodie, on the phone, she was especially excited because Riley was her first granddaughter. "Oh, that's wonderful," she exclaimed. "What's her name?"

"Riley Rae," I said.

After a silence, Dodie said: "Well, I guess there's nothing we can do about that now, is there?"

It was sweet, but we understood. If Kerry's mom had had her way, she would have named all the kids in the family. If Riley didn't quite fit the bill, that was okay with us.

My mom was on a plane as soon as Riley was born and, as with Kelty, she was a big help, keeping the house clean and food on the table while I did my best to adjust to a brand new routine with two small children. Kelty loved his baby sister, but he definitely noticed a change in the family dynamic. He no longer had our undivided attention. He started waking up during the night and would come in and wake us up, too. Most nights, I would lie down with him in his bed and sing him the Irish lullaby "Too-Ra-Loo-Ra-Loo-Ral" until he fell back to sleep.

Like her brother, Riley didn't take to breastfeeding. In those first few weeks, she vomited so much that Mom and I took her to the hospital one day to have her checked out. She was fine, but as we were pulling into the driveway back home, we saw Kelty sitting high up in a tree in our yard. When he spotted us, he promptly fell out of the tree and split open his chin. We had to turn the car around and go straight back to the hospital, where he needed stitches to close the gash.

Even though he was a rambunctious kid, Kelty seldom had health problems aside from the usual kids' stuff. Riley, though, had problems from the start. At eight months old, she began having so much trouble breathing that we took her to emergency. The doctor told us she had asthma. That first spell was the start of a pattern. We never knew when an asthma attack was coming, so we were always on the alert, Riley's puffers and medications at the ready.

At about eighteen months, while Kerry was away on a fishing trip up north, Riley had a severe attack. The emergency room doctor began going through the usual routine— admit her, treat her, send her home. But this time, a nurse took me aside and quietly suggested that Riley should be transferred to Children's Hospital in Vancouver. Riley, she implied without saying so, needed more attention than she was getting. The doctor resisted my request but I insisted, and eventually Riley was taken by ambulance to Children's. Within two hours she was in intensive care on a respirator, in an induced coma. It's hard to explain the feeling of seeing your baby hooked up to machines and ivs and tubes. Riley was helpless, and so was I. They were doing everything they could, but she didn't seem to be getting better. Since Kerry was out in the bush, I couldn't get in touch with him at first. All I could do was stay by Riley's side and try to comfort her. One morning, a nurse came into Riley's hospital room and told me they had summoned a priest.

"Mrs. Dennehy," the priest said to me, "you're going to have to figure out how to deal with Riley's death."

I told the medical staff she wasn't going to die. I would will Riley to live. And I did. I don't know how, but I stuck by her side and slowly, so slowly, she got better. It took three weeks before she was out of the woods, and she needed to be weaned off the drugs, which were hard on her little body and had even caused her to hallucinate. She was brave through it all, but she would cry and say, "Mommy, Mommy, no more pokies" because she hated the needles. Because she had been in bed for so long and the drugs were so strong, her recovery included painstaking physical therapy rehabilitation. She also had to take steroids to build up her strength. Riley came home from the hospital in a wheelchair, transferring to a walker until her legs became strong enough for her to walk on her own again. It all seemed too much for such a little thing, but there was something in Riley that spoke to an inner strength and determination, and she never gave up.

We went through life-threatening asthma attacks eight more times over the next few years, wearing a rut in the road back and forth to Children's Hospital. Each time, Riley would be near death but would find something within herself that allowed her to fight back. On one of her hospital stays, I ran into an acquaintance whose young daughter, battling a rare respiratory illness, was a patient on the same floor as Riley. The two of us often took breaks together, talking about our girls and their fighting spirits. It was comforting to share my thoughts with someone going through the same kind of crisis. Late one night, when Riley was especially fussy, I went to the nurses' station to get some advice. I noticed a commotion in a nearby room and realized that my friend's daughter had died. She and her husband were just standing there holding each other, and it was so sad to witness their grief. I went back to be with Riley and sat there in the dark wondering how these things happen. I still had my daughter, and I was lucky, but I felt guilty, too. It didn't seem right that my daughter was alive and theirs was not.

Riley's health troubles didn't end with asthma. She developed severe food allergies early on to such staples as fish and eggs and nuts. We had to watch every little thing she ate. Those first few years were hard on all of us, but especially on Kelty, who was increasingly conscious that we were spending a lot of our time with his sick sister. He got angry and jealous and would sometimes complain, but we knew it was because he didn't understand. We did our best to make sure he knew how much we loved him.

And there was no question that the big brother loved his little sister. He was always kissing and hugging her. Once, when he and Riley were playing Sleeping Beauty in the yard, he gave her a big smooch on the lips. But he had just eaten a peanut butter sandwich, and within minutes we were again rushing Riley to the hospital. We could never have cakes at birthday parties because of the eggs, so we'd have Jell-O cakes instead. The kids eventually grew accustomed to the restrictions, but Kerry and I remained constantly vigilant.

Kelty was going to preschool by now, and when he was five, he began to play hockey at the Hollyburn Country Club. He not only loved the game but was a good player, earning a reputation as a gifted skater. Both kids were very active, always looking for that next adventure. When they weren't outside careening down the driveway on trikes or bicycles, they were playing in the fort we'd built in the back-yard beside the creek.

Although they were close, they developed that traditional love/hate relationship that siblings have. Kelty was madcap. Riley was a thinker, but she was more of a dare-devil than her brother once she made up her mind to do something. They'd be fighting one second, and then a moment later they'd be screaming with laughter.

The two of them spent hours playing with Riley's Fisher-Price kitchen, and Kelty would follow me all over the house with his toy vacuum cleaner when I was doing housework. When he wanted to be off on his own, it was all about his Transformers and his Super Mario game. For Riley, it was her trolls, those ugly dolls with the wild, brightly coloured hair. They were everywhere in her room and all over the house. She had a "trollie" blanket, and every time we took her to the hospital, we had to take her trollie blanket, too. She also loved Sally, a floppy baby doll. Riley was definitely a girlie-girl. I was in Las Vegas on business one year when Kerry called to say Riley was back in hospital with a bad bout of asthma. She was in the ICU and wasn't doing well. I headed right for the airport and while waiting for my flight, went into a kiosk and bought her a doll. It wasn't really a doll to play with, because it was porcelain and had a wind-up mechanism that played the Beatles song "Michelle," but it was all I could find. Riley loved it, but after she recovered and we were back home, I wouldn't let her play with it because it was too fragile. Every once in a while she would ask if she could hold the "beautiful baby," and we'd sit together and talk about how lovely she was.

Riley's hospital visits became routine. Sometimes she would be there a week at a time, and when that happened during the school year, we'd have to get her work brought into the hospital so she wouldn't fall behind in class.

Jo had left us as nanny, and when we found Imelda, it was like we had struck gold. She was an open-hearted Filipina woman who loved the kids. She spoiled them terribly, and of course they loved her back. She was so helpful in keeping Kelty busy during those rough years of Riley's sickness and frequent hospital stays. She became like a member of the family and would stay that way even after the kids were grown.

In 1987, Kerry left Earl's to strike out on his own, starting a small food distribution company. It was a complicated business, and after two years he decided to try something else. He got his commercial real estate licence and went to work for Royal LePage in the downtown core.

The kids, meanwhile, were busy with karate, swimming, and skating lessons. Both of them were naturally athletic, and they were more involved with sports than with the arts, clearly the influence of their mom and dad. They were good at everything they tried. They were competitive, too, though Kelty wanted to be the centre of attention, whereas Riley was happy to hang back and let him hog the limelight. They were funny kids, imbued with a sense of humour that kept us laughing. They would leave little notes around the house, as well as drawings and poems. If we had a squabble with them over chores or something they should have known better than to do, they would write a letter apologizing and telling us they loved us.

They were, in every way, amazing.

One of our favourite annual events was Riley's birthday. Because it was in July, we'd have outdoor parties with apple bobbing and spoon races and lots of kids running around the local park. Kelty was stuck with indoor celebrations for his birthday in November, but we tried to make them just as much fun.

Both kids had been on skis since the age of three, so we thought it made sense for us to get a place in Whistler, a ski resort a two-and-a-half-hour drive from Vancouver. We would go up every weekend and in summer spend hours hiking and golfing and riding our bikes along the trails. We loved the place, and in 1996 we decided to move there permanently.

It might have seemed odd to give up our life in West Vancouver when things were going so well. The kids were settled in school, had great friends, and were busy with all their activities. I was at a job I loved, working from home and travelling all over the western region with IBM. Kerry was busy with his real estate. But the truth was that, as the kids grew older, I was increasingly unsettled by the West Vancouver lifestyle, with its insular trappings of wealth. Once, when we were at a hockey wrap-up party in a beautiful house in the area with a swimming pool, Kelty said off-handedly, "Mom, we could never have a wrap-up party. We don't have a nice enough house." That set off my parental alarm bells. I worried that, no matter how we tried to counteract it, our kids were being unduly influenced by their surroundings. Kerry shared my concern.

One weekend, I was up at our Whistler place hosting a group of women friends from Winnipeg, when I drove by the Nicklaus North development. It was like a moonscape, no trees, just dirt, but there was something about the location that pulled me in. The beauty of the place, with the water and the distant mountains and the wild blue horizon, was magical. There was a construction trailer on the site, so I went and looked at the map of the planned community. The houses were modern, with an elegant, woodsy look, and meandered along the golf course adjacent to Green Lake. I knew it was for us.

Riley was always game for something new, and Kelty was thrilled. He was sad to leave his friends, but he couldn't wait to live someplace he could ski all the time. We sold the house on Hadden Drive, put our stuff in storage, bought a lot on Nicklaus North Boulevard, and in September 1996 moved into our condo while our house was being built. The kids were enrolled in Myrtle Philip Community School—Kelty in Grade 7 and Riley in Grade 4. I needed an office, so I took over a corner of the kids' bedroom, which had bunk beds. We always kept a spare bedroom for guests, and the kids didn't seem to mind Mom sharing their space.

Whistler is a small town with a strong sense of community. There are only about ten thousand year-round residents. Riley found her new best friend, Britt Gibbons, within a nanosecond, and they were soul sisters from that moment on. Kelty found kindred spirits in new best buddies like Pat Sanderson and Trevor O'Reilly. Kerry took a job with Sussex Realty and got involved right away with the local hockey association, coaching and playing in the men's hockey league. Both the kids learned to snowboard, and they played hockey, too. Riley even joined a boys' team. Kelty and Kerry did the Whistler-to-Squamish mountain bike ride through the trails off the highway, and father and son spent a lot of time on the golf course. Kelty would get frustrated when his dad played a better round, but it was just part of his personality. Kerry and I skied and hiked, and Kerry often went off on canoeing trips with his friends. For outdoor enthusiasts like us, Whistler was paradise.

Sadly, Imelda hadn't come with us to Whistler. By then, she had married her boyfriend from the Philippines, settled in Vancouver, and had three children of her own. But our connection was so strong that we continued to stay in touch. We certainly missed her—me especially—but our little family unit was tight and happy.

We still spent as much of July and August as we could at my family cabin outside Winnipeg and the Dennehy cottage at Victoria Beach. For the kids, it was the best of both worlds: swimming and driving the farm's tractor with my dad or piling into his van, which they called the Yellow Bird, to head up the road for a lunch of foot-long hot dogs. The beach was just as much fun. There were no cars allowed in the Victoria Beach area, so everyone had to leave their vehicles in a big communal parking lot and take "taxis," old panelled station wagons that transported vacationers and their stuff to the several hundred cottages on the lakefront. The only other mode of transport was bicycles, which everyone pedalled to pick up groceries and visit friends. There was even a little seasonal newspaper, the *Victoria Herald*, filled with local gossip.

Kerry and I had both been raised in households overflowing with kids and pets, so it seemed natural that our home would be the same. The kids had turtles and gerbils, and they were always catching spiders and other creatures and housing them in jars. We were dog people, and a favourite over the years was Kelly, a cairn/poodle cross. Kelly was queen of the house; she imagined herself a bull mastiff when she could better fit in a shoebox. She had hypoallergenic fur, which was important for Riley's allergies. The kids called her Schmee, and she insisted on sleeping in their beds when she wasn't following them everywhere or chasing her tail out on the fairway. We almost lost her once, when she ate a stash of chocolate, but she recovered and lived to charm us for many more years.

If life could ever be perfect, our lives together were surely close.

(3)

. . . .

Kelty

. . . .

KELTY HAD BEEN handsome from the moment he was
born, sweet-faced with a touch of freckles across his nose,
his soft blond baby hair turning into a thick shock of dark
as he grew from toddler to teen. His bright blue eyes carried a perpetual twinkle, and he could make us laugh with
a mere sideways glance. But it was in his teens that Kelty
really bloomed. He loved being the centre of attention, and
his big circle of friends would head out snowboarding or
gather in our sports room, playing pool and eating pizza, the
house full of the glorious din of the raucous young. Kelty
was also a bit of a fashion plate, and he liked to wear the ball
caps and tees, the jackets and sneakers that teen boys of the
day favoured, all emblazoned with trendy logos and cheeky
inscriptions. His ski and snowboard gear was the best,
updated as often as we indulged him. Although he liked
girls, and flirted with the notion of dating, he didn't have
a serious girlfriend so much as a wide circle of girlfriends,
part of the crowd traipsing in and out of our house. If Kelty

was attracted to some of Riley's friends, the reverse was certainly true at times. The town was so small that everyone knew each other, and teenage romance was inevitable.

Our new house was spacious, 2,900 square feet, with an airy, vaulted main level that featured fir ceiling beams and polished maple floors. A grand stone gas fireplace dominated the great room. The kitchen had a granite island flanked by stools, and the adjoining dining room easily accommodated our overflowing get-togethers with family and friends. The cedar deck that stretched across the back of the house overlooked the fifteenth hole of the Nicklaus North Golf Course, picture-perfect Green Lake, and the mountains beyond. The house was multi-level, with a main floor master bedroom and bath, an open loft office for me, and another bathroom and small office on the landing.

The ground floor space belonged to Kelty and Riley. It was custom designed, with two bedrooms, each with window seats, and a shared bathroom in the hallway. The games room had shuffleboard, a pool table, and a dart board, and it opened onto the lower deck, where the steaming hot tub offered a spellbinding view over the lake. The mud room that led to the garage was always a tangled riot of jackets, boots, gym bags, ski equipment, and hastily shed shoes and socks. From the day we moved in, the house was full of noise and laughter, banging doors and kids hollering from floor to floor. The radio and CDs blared day and night, with a television in one of the rooms often on full volume. It was all music to my ears.

When Kelty decided in Grade 7 that he wanted to start a band because he'd been playing the drums in music class, we were surprised. Kerry and I went to his school concert, and we were astonished to see our son playing the drums with some skill. When people came up to us afterward and said they hadn't known that Kelty played the drums, we had to admit that we hadn't either. He tinkered with the band notion for a while but then decided the drums weren't really his thing.

Riley had taken some dance classes while we were living in West Vancouver, and early on, she caught the acting bug that had bitten many of her cousins. She was in all the plays in her elementary school, acting as the Wicked Witch of the West in one production. She also taught herself to play a little guitar a few years later. But she was such a great athlete that most of her time was spent playing hockey, basketball, and volleyball. And, of course, snowboarding.

As with most busy families, the heart of our house was the kitchen. It was where everyone gathered, hopping up on the bar stools for breakfast or plopping down after school to bug me about what I was making for dinner. Kelty, especially, was a food hound. If something special like Thanksgiving dinner was on the menu, he was less concerned about the turkey than he was about what he called the details. "Mom," he would say, "what are we having with that? What are the vegetables? Is there wild rice?" He had been the same with Imelda, always asking her to make special Filipino food, especially her noodle dishes.

Aside from the obligatory Disneyland visits, we mostly did short spur-of-the-moment excursions with the kids. Once, I took Riley and her friend Claire down to Seattle by train, and we had a wonderful time. Kerry and Kelty often headed off on weekend fishing and camping trips. I would occasionally fly one of the kids out to join me when I travelled for work. Kelty and I spent one weekend together in Toronto, a memorable mother-son experience.

We visited the Hockey Hall of Fame, went to a Toronto Maple Leafs game, and talked about hockey and life over a big steak dinner. I remember looking across the table and thinking that my beautiful little boy was growing into a fine young man.

In September 1997, the newly built Whistler Secondary School opened its doors, and Kelty started Grade 8 there. It was the only high school in town, and for the community kids graduating from elementary to secondary, there was a new world around the corner. Kelty was excited about it, walking the wide dirt path that wound through the woods from our house to the school every day, laughing and chatting with best pals like Pat and Trevor, their whole lives unfolding before them, a future full of adventures.

By thirteen, Kelty had been playing hockey for half his life. He wasn't a big kid, but he was fast on skates, with a lot of finesse, and he was known as a thinker on the ice, always ahead of the next move. He played forward, the number seventeen on his jersey flashing around the rink. (His hockey hero was Eric Lindros, and once when I ran into Lindros, I had him sign a personalized autograph that Kelty cherished.) He practised religiously several times a week with the Whistler Minor Hockey League, and he was always suited up and ready for the league's weekly game.

Like most players his age who exhibited talent, Kelty fancied himself a hockey star. Bolstered by the blinkers of youth, he assumed that he would one day be discovered by an NHL scout and drafted to the big leagues. So it was no surprise to Kerry or me when Kelty started bugging us to let him get more serious about his hockey career.

One day, out it came: "Mom, I really want to go to Notre Dame."

Athol Murray College of Notre Dame was in Wilcox, Saskatchewan—from our perspective, an awfully long way from home. But Kelty didn't care. Not only was Notre Dame a renowned private preparatory institution, it was also famous for its athletic programs. It was known across the country as the home of the Hounds, its celebrated hockey team, and it boasted a winning legacy of national hockey championships and alumni that included NHL players Russ Courtnall and Gary Leeman.

Kelty wanted to be a Hound.

He knew that it wouldn't be easy—on any front. Notre Dame had a reputation for strict adherence to its high standards, from religion to sports. In the early days, students had slept in bunkhouses without heat, a toughening-up exercise that later translated into an unwavering expectation that students adhere to the edicts of community involvement and leadership and to the values that are the hallmarks of good character.

We knew that Kelty's zeal about going to Notre Dame was tempered by some apprehension. He would be leaving his friends and his family, his comfort zone, and we talked about how that might make it a drastic change. He was so focussed on ultimately becoming an NHL player that nothing else seemed to matter. I wasn't convinced, but as he always did, Kelty started working on me, knowing that I would eventually cave and that my acquiescence would make his dad an easier sell on the idea. Kerry was the perfect counter to my impulsiveness—he tended to think longer and harder about things, especially when it came to money, and private school meant money. Kelty was good at persuading us, though, and we finally agreed that he could go. He applied and was accepted, and we enrolled him for Grade 10. All four of us drove out to Saskatchewan in August 1998 to get him settled.

Kelty's first year went reasonably well. He joined the school's golf team and made some good friends, but the school work was a challenge, more stringent than he was used to, and he would often phone home to talk about how things were going. The hardest part, we knew, was when he realized that though he had been a top player in Whistler, he was now in another league. As a Notre Dame Hound, he was a small fish in a big pond stocked with some of the best young players in the country. When Kelty didn't make the A team or even the B team at Notre Dame but was instead put on the C team, it was a blow. Even if he wasn't gaining a name through hockey, he had become a popular fixture around the Notre Dame campus. Everyone called him Doctor D., the good-natured peacemaker his classmates would seek out for advice. Nonetheless, when he asked us if he could return to Whistler Secondary for Grade 11, we told him he could. We wanted him to be happy, and we missed him and wanted him home with us.

Back in Whistler, Kelty pulled up his socks and began to thrive again, working so hard at school that he was the only boy to make the Grade 11 honour roll. He was proud to be up on that stage, the only boy with all the smart girls, once again the centre of attention. Sitting in the audience, we were more proud of him than ever.

That Christmas, we decided to take the kids on a two-week cruise through the Panama Canal. We went with our neighbours, the Richmonds, and their friends the Thomases. Altogether, there were fourteen of us, and most of the youngsters in the group were the same ages as Kelty and Riley. It seemed like the ideal vacation—lots of kids and lots of things for them to do. It was our first cruise as a family, and we were excited. We flew to Puerto Vallarta and spent Christmas Day there before boarding the ship and heading south through the canal to Cartagena, Colombia.

Visits to the ports along the way kept us not only entertained but also busy from morning to night. We hardly saw the kids, except when we met for meals to talk about the day. At first, Kelty was his usual social self, jumping around in the pool, teasing the girls and partying with the other teens in our group. He was into rap and break dancing, having spent hours honing his skills in our garage with his friend Jeff, and he showed up at the start of each day wearing his favourite baseball hat and stylish street clothes, full of confidence and mischief.

And then everything changed.

One evening toward the end of the trip, we were in our cabin getting ready for dinner when Kelty turned to his dad and said, "I'm going to throw myself off the cruise ship." It was as if a switch had gone off—he was suddenly a completely different boy, withdrawn, agitated, and fretful. We didn't know what was going on, but Kerry calmed Kelty down and said he'd stay with him in the cabin while Riley and I met the others for dinner. Back in the cabin, though, Kelty didn't settle down. He told his dad that he didn't want to eat, he didn't want to see anyone. He was insistent, and it was so unlike him. Worried, Kerry called the ship's doctor, who came and gave Kelty a sedative, assuring Kerry that it was nothing more than an anxiety attack. The shot seemed to work, and Kelty slept a bit.

But his mood, his anxiousness, continued for the next two days. Kelty talked about feeling overwhelmed, unable to control or understand his emotions. Kerry stayed in the cabin with him, ordering soup and cheese sandwiches and desperately trying to keep our son on an even keel. But it was a scary time. "Dad," Kelty would say, "I don't know what's wrong with me. This thing just grabbed me." Kerry thought it might help to involve the ship's priest; he knew that Kelty believed in God and had become more interested in Catholicism while at Notre Dame. The priest came and talked to Kelty, and that did seem to help.

During a stopover in the San Blas Islands of Panama, Kelty joined the other kids in a volleyball game they had planned. He was slightly embarrassed about what had happened and didn't want to talk about it anymore. But although he appeared more composed, he definitely wasn't the Kelty we knew. His heart wasn't in the game, and his usual gregarious self had been replaced by a quiet, subdued boy we barely recognized. We were very worried. Kelty had always been a bit of a fretter, but he had never acted like this. We now know he was exhibiting signs of a deep-seated depression.

The cruise was winding down, but before heading home, we stayed overnight in San Diego, taking in the zoo and the local sights. Things almost seemed back to normal. Kelty was in good spirits, and we had a wonderful family time there. Back in Whistler, we settled into our routines. Kelty seemed happy to be playing hockey, going to parties, working at the golf course, and hanging out with his friends. But there was no question that something in our son had changed. The carefree part of his personality had been replaced by a drive for perfection, a need to get the best grades, play the best hockey, shoot the best golf score. Looking back, I think the switch was tripped after his Grade 11 honour roll achievement. Once he'd had a taste of academic excellence and the accolades that could bring, he wanted more challenges than he felt Whistler Secondary could offer. He asked us if he could return to Notre Dame in September for Grade 12.

Once again, his argument was convincing. It wasn't just for the hockey, he told us, but for the scholastics. Kelty had always been a boy more likely to take the easier path, relying on his charm and hockey skills, but here he was talking about going to law school after graduation from Notre Dame, about applying to Bishop's College, a small, high-level, sports-oriented university in Lennoxville, Quebec. He had thought hard about what he wanted to do with his life, and this, he said with much conviction, was the path he wanted to take.

Kerry and I were beyond proud. The incident on our vacation simmered in the back of our minds, but it seemed our sixteen-year-old son had turned a corner and was growing up, taking responsibility, and exhibiting ambition about his future. As much as Kelty was the goofball of the family, he had never been the kind of teen who drank too much or who would drink and drive or even party late into the night. He worked part-time, earning his own spending money, and he was the one who drove his friends home or made them stay with us if they had been drinking too much. He was a good kid, and it made sense to us that he was on this track. As much as we wanted him home with us, we felt that as parents we needed to support his goals. We enrolled him again in Notre Dame.

For Riley, Kelty's spell on our vacation, and his newfound conviction about his future, were all just part of what was happening in the family. She was a teenager, too, and as much as she loved her brother, she didn't mind having the house to herself. She loved high school and was immersed in the social swirl. She and Britt were still inseparable; they were birds of a feather and had been since elementary school, always up to shenanigans. Their time in Brownies had lasted no longer than a heartbeat; they were kicked out for giggling at the wrong times, like over the fake campfire at circle time in the gym. And although they vowed to be best friends forever, they occasionally squabbled. It wasn't unusual for me to phone Britt's mom, Colleen, and say, "Okay, is the war between Britain and France on or off?" Riley was busy playing hockey and snowboarding, and she was starting to take more than a passing interest in boys. Her affections included Kelty's best friend, Trevor, and she dated Thomas, a family friend's son, for about a year before he moved away to go to school. It wasn't that she wasn't engaged in what was happening with Kelty; it was just that she was wrapped up in her own life.

I was nervous about Kelty's return to Notre Dame. I remembered how homesick he had been before and how he had seemed lost in the crowd out there. The incident on the cruise ship weighed heavily on my mind. I reminded Kelty of how he had struggled at Notre Dame, but he was adamant: "Mom, I need to be tougher, I need to be challenged, I have to do this." He was so determined.

Kerry drove Kelty to Saskatchewan in August 2000, a long father-son trip with open stretches of highway perfect for talking. At some point, as he told me later, Kerry let Kelty take the wheel, but he became alarmed at his careless driving. When Kerry told him to slow down, Kelty just looked over at his dad and shrugged. It was so out of character, as was an incident a few months later when Kerry made a visit to the school to watch Kelty play hockey with his

Notre Dame team. When Kelty told him, "Dad, I'm going to get in a fight for you," Kerry was stunned. Kelty had never been aggressive in any way; on the ice, he had always exhibited his talent through his skating finesse. Kerry said "No, Kelt," but Kelty did it anyway, as if he was trying to prove something to his dad.

Kerry and I chalked these things up to the transitions Kelty was making on the road to maturity, the rocky time all teenagers go through as they make the break from the protective cocoon of their parents. We had kept a close eye on our children's friends and their activities, but we had no idea that the breakdown on the ship and Kelty's overt drive for perfection, his speeding and fighting, were all signs of the depression that was tightening its grip on him.

Kelty seemed to love being back at Notre Dame for his senior year, and he checked in with us regularly on the phone. He was doing well in everything except math, and he told Kerry about one math teacher who had thrown a test down on Kelty's desk and said derisively, "Good luck with this one." We know now that sometimes the smallest things can trigger anxiety, act as catalysts for the dormant demons that feed depression. Sometime later, Kerry would take that teacher aside and remind him that words can do much harm.

Kelty came home that Christmas, and on the surface he seemed happy with his life. He quickly took up with his Whistler friends, hit the mountains, and reconnected with Riley. Feeling it was time for another family vacation, we booked an all-inclusive trip to Puerto Vallarta with the families who had joined us on the cruise the year before. Things started out well. The parents met every night for cocktail hour just before dinner while the kids were busy on the beach, parasailing and partying in the banana boat that sailed back and forth offshore. Kelty was once again the ringleader of the group.

One night at dinner, Kelty said out of the blue, "C'mon, Mom, let's dance." It was special, me and my seventeen-year-old son twirling together around the dance floor, and it was so like Kelty. He was the rare kind of teenager who would run up to me in front of his friends, give me a big hug, and tell me I was the best mom in the world. I had always said we were soulmates, and I never felt it more than that night while we were dancing.

New Year's Eve is a huge celebration in Mexico, and we agreed to gather in the dining room to celebrate and ring in the new year. At some point, I realized Kelty wasn't there. When I went up to the room he was sharing with Riley, I found him in bed. It startled me. I said: "Kelts, what are you doing? It's New Year's Eve."

"Mom, it's okay," he said. "I just want to be safe. I'm fine, don't worry. I just feel that this is where I need to be right now."

My alarm bells went off. I found Kerry and told him, and when he went to check on our son, Kelty said the same thing. "I'm fine, Dad. I'm just tired. I'm okay." Kelty eventually fell asleep, but we kept checking on him all night.

We weren't home in Whistler long before it was time for Kelty to go back to Notre Dame. I took him to the airport, but we were early, so we decided to have something to eat. At one point, he looked at me and said: "Mom, I just don't feel that good about going back to school."

I was surprised. He had been doing so well since he'd returned in September, and he hadn't said a word to Kerry or me about not wanting to return until that moment. I told him I sometimes felt like that when it was time to return to work after a vacation, and that sometimes we just had to push through it and do our best. I was sure he wasn't the only high school student, the only Notre Dame student, who struggled to measure up to high standards, I said. He nodded, and then it was time for his flight. He walked toward the security gate and then came back out and waved to me, doing it several times. It rattled me a bit—I couldn't help but think, "Is my boy okay?" I just didn't know. I worried on the drive back to Whistler.

That night, Kelty phoned me from the dorm pay phone. He was crying. "Mom, I don't know how to explain this, but I was on the airplane and I had these terrible, terrible thoughts. It was kind of like I was on this roller coaster, and I'd kind of go into the pit of my stomach. Mom, I don't want to feel like that. How come I'm feeling like that? Mom, make me better."

A prickle of fear shot down my back. "Kelts, settle down, just settle down." I told him to hold on, and from our other line I phoned his house parent in the dorm, related what was going on, and asked him to go and be with Kelty. The house parent phoned me back to say that Kelty had been anxious at first, but now everything seemed okay.

After that, we talked to Kelty every day. Sometimes he was in a great mood, telling us about the hockey games on his schedule, but other days he wasn't himself. At our request, Notre Dame arranged for him to see a therapist in Regina. He prescribed Paxil, a widely used antidepressant, and Ativan, another common prescription used to treat anxiety. Kelty didn't like taking medication of any kind—he hid the pill bottles from his friends—but he told us the drugs calmed him and allowed him to concentrate. It was, like everything else for Kelty, about being normal. If he needed Paxil and Ativan to feel normal, then that's all that mattered.

In late January, Kerry went out to Notre Dame. He convinced Kelty to start keeping a journal, which he hoped would help our son better understand how he was feeling. We felt we were doing everything we could—the school was aware of Kelty's fragility, he was seeing a Notre Dame counsellor, he had been prescribed the appropriate medication, and we were monitoring him daily. Still, when it was time for Kerry to leave, he did so reluctantly.

A week later, I was on a business trip in Toronto when Kelty phoned me. His voice was filled with the kind of anguish you never want to hear from your children. "Mom, I need you. I need you so much."

Again, the prickle of fear. "Kelty," I said, "I'm coming."

I immediately flew to Regina, drove to the school, and took Kelty with me to my hotel. His midterm exams were coming up, and he was worried about how he would do. It was also the weekend of the school's winter dance, and he wanted to go. We decided to study together and then went shopping for some new clothes so that he could look sharp at the dance. I dropped him off at the school for the Friday night party, but on the way back to the hotel I couldn't stop asking myself: "How can my beautiful boy be suffering so much? Why can't I take away his pain?"

The next morning I had an appointment with the therapist the school had recommended Kelty see. The counsellor greeted me at his office mid-shave, as if that was perfectly normal. He was too casual for me—and unprofessional. Things didn't improve when the first thing he said to me was, "Do you think Kelty is gay?"

I was furious. "I couldn't care less if he's gay," I snapped. "That's not what we're talking about. I want to know what's going on with my child."

"Well, he's probably gay. That's his problem."

That's all the counsellor could say. After I'd asked him a few more questions, I decided I didn't want Kelty to see him again.

After the disastrous appointment, I picked up Kelty at his dorm. He'd enjoyed the dance and partying with his friends, he said. As we continued talking, I was surprised by the number of questions he asked about our family history, wondering what people like his great-grandfather had been like. He told me that he liked going to the school chapel, because he found comfort and quiet there. A girl he liked was always there, too. "That's kind of a neat sign, eh, Mom?"

Over the course of the day, I met with everyone around Kelty, including the head of the school and the school priest. We all knew that many teens struggle with anxiety through their school years, that the pressure and the expectations are often too much to handle. The school was not unfamiliar with the phenomenon of teen depression or with its widespread effect.

That night over dinner, Kelty asked, "Mom, do you think Dad would mind if I wanted to be a priest?"

"Kelty, Dad will be fine with whatever you want to be. He just wants you to be happy."

"Well, I think I might want to go into the army. What do you think about that? What do you think Dad would say?"

It was strange, so extreme—from a priest to a soldier—but I told him we would support him in whatever he decided to do, that we just wanted what was best for him.

Then he started talking about Bishop's and wanting to be a lawyer. He was all over the map, taking stabs at everything, looking ahead but also looking for approval.

Kelty stayed with me at my hotel in Regina, and I drove him back to school on Monday. When I dropped him off, he told me he was fine. He was going to study for his midterms, and he was looking forward to an upcoming hockey game in Morden, Manitoba, because all four of his grandparents were driving in from Winnipeg to watch him play. I headed for the airport and flew home.

Two days later, he phoned.

"Mom, I have to come home."

I was relieved. I knew intuitively that Kelty wasn't okay, that he needed to be near us, that school didn't matter at that point. He flew to Vancouver on February 14. Our friends the Thomases, who had been on our recent family trips, picked him up at the airport and kept him overnight. Kerry and I went down to get him the next morning.

Whistler was caught up in Valentine's Day fever when Kelty got back, and Riley was looking forward to a big party planned for that evening. She knew Kelty wasn't doing well since we had talked to her about it, and although she seemed to understand, she was immersed in her own life like any teenager. Her uncle Clancy, a terrific photographer, was coming to town and planned to take pictures of Riley and all her friends. Being a fifteen-year-old girl, that was all she could think about.

Kelty was happy to be home. He had brought his books from school because he wanted to study, and it cheered him up to reconnect with his pals. On his first day back he called Pat and Trevor, and the whole gang converged on our place, playing pool and having fun. A kind of normalcy had taken hold, but only for a moment. Kerry and I were in our bedroom watching television when suddenly Kelty was standing in the doorway, tears streaming down his face. "Mom,

I don't want to have these terrible thoughts. Please, please help me not have these terrible thoughts."

We asked his friends to go and then tucked him into our bed with us. I hugged him as he cried, wanting only to take away his pain. I kept saying, "I will take care of you. I will take care of you. I promise. I promise." I sang him "Too-Ra-Loo-Ra-Loo-Ral" and hung on tight to him all through the night.

The next day, Kerry took Kelty to the Whistler medical clinic. The doctor knew about Kelty and the struggles he had been having. He gave him some more medication for his anxiety and recommended he see a local therapist right away. Kelty didn't want to talk to a therapist again, but Kerry insisted, so he went for a few sessions.

Kerry had been planning to join me on a business trip to Florida, but now that our boy needed us, we decided not to go. Kelty was upset, insisting that we not change our plans. We were equally insistent about not leaving him. Kelty asked me to read his journal, the one his dad had encouraged him to start writing the month before. It was such a private thing to share, and I could tell it was important to him, so I agreed.

I sat on his bed and flipped through the pages. He'd written about what he was going through, about his terrible thoughts and how he wondered if he would ever be normal again. He knew he had to try to get better for his family, he wrote; he would do anything for me and his dad and his sister. He was getting better, he said, and he was looking forward to the future, to going back to school. It was all there in his familiar, confident handwriting.

I was still reading his journal when he came into the room. "See, Mom? I'm getting better. Let Dad and me stay here together. I think it will be good for you to go on your business trip. You'll call, and we can talk."

I wrestled with it but then decided it would be a good chance for Kerry and Kelty to bond even more. Kerry agreed. I realize now that Kelty's intuitiveness was on high alert. Having me read his journal, he knew, would help calm my fear.

Once away, I phoned home every day. Kelty seemed to be having a great time snowboarding with his friends, and that put me somewhat at ease. A few days after I left, on a sparkling Monday morning, Kerry decided to go skiing with the Patersons, friends of ours who were in town. He and Kelty agreed that Kelty would stay behind and study. The agreement with Notre Dame was that as long as Kelty finished his school work for the year, there was a possibility he could still graduate. That meant hitting the books at home.

We later learned that when his dad left for the mountain that morning, Kelty put on his coat and left the house, walking down the block and through the woods to Whistler High School, taking the winding path he had walked so many times with his friends. He spent some time wandering around the school, reconnecting with his friends and teachers, greeting them warmly and chatting about what was going on in his life.

On his way back home he ran into Riley, who was heading to school for the day. He was upset and crying, and it shocked her. "Kelt, what's wrong?" she asked him, but he simply put his arms around her and said, "Riley, I love you."

She couldn't have known it then, but he was saying goodbye.

Riley carried on to school, and Kelty went home. When his dad phoned later that morning to see how he was doing,

Kelty assured him he was fine, that he was sitting on the couch studying. An hour or so later, Kerry called again, and the phone rang and rang. When Kelty finally picked it up, he was in tears. "Dad, I love you, I love you."

He kept saying it over and over, and Kerry knew Kelty was in trouble. He begged him to hold on, said he was coming down the mountain as fast as he could and would be right there. But Kelty just kept saying, "No, dad, I love you, I love you, I love you."

Kerry phoned 911 and told them to dispatch an ambulance to the house. He asked them not to frighten Kelty with sirens. He skied hard down the mountain, hailed a taxi at the base, and arrived at the house just as the ambulance was pulling up. The paramedics all ran into the house following Kerry, who was bounding up the stairs, calling "Kelt, Kelt, Kelt." He found our beautiful son limply hanging from the rafters in the loft, a garden hose wrapped around his neck.

They took him down. Kelty was alive but unconscious, and they sped him by ambulance to the Whistler clinic, where it was quickly decided to transport him by helicopter to Royal Columbian Hospital in New Westminster. Kerry had been frantically trying to reach me, and when I returned to my room to get ready for dinner I saw the message light flashing on the phone. I phoned Kerry's cell.

"Ginny," he said, "Kelty has had a very bad accident."

The prickle again. "What do you mean, he's had an accident?"

"Ginny, he tried to take his life. You need to get home."

It was as if I was outside my body, listening in on someone else's conversation. It couldn't be real. My mind was racing, and I suddenly remembered how earlier in the day when I was lying outside by the pool, I had felt a sudden jolt. I now know that it was Kelty.

I knew I had to get home, but I couldn't think how I would do that. I called my friend Barb in Toronto's IBM office and told her what had happened. She arranged a flight for the next morning, then contacted one of our business partners and his wife, who were at the conference. They came and stayed with me through the night. I couldn't sleep. How could this be? How could this be happening? My beautiful boy. My beautiful boy. A car picked me up at 6 AM and took me to the airport. I had a stopover somewhere but don't recall where. I was in a fog, anxious to be home but so afraid of what I would find there. When I finally landed in Vancouver, Air Canada quickly ushered me through customs to my sister Cath and her husband, Rick. Cath wrapped her arms around me, her love like a comforting blanket.

We drove directly to Royal Columbian.

I walked into the hospital room, and there was my Kelty, hooked up to tubes and surrounded by machines that were quietly pumping and beeping, breathing for him, keeping him alive. His eyes were closed, and he looked so handsome and peaceful. He had been snowboarding the day before, and his face was sunburned, ruddy and healthy. But when I got closer, I could see the burns around his neck.

Guilt washed over me. I now know that he had planned everything, that he made sure I wouldn't be there when he chose to end his life. He knew his dad was stronger and could handle it better. He was trying to protect me, even as I was trying to protect him.

Kerry was in the room, and Riley was there with Britt and Britt's mother, Colleen. I was grateful to know they had been looking after Riley; I was so lost in grief I could barely put one foot in front of the other. Cath and Rick stayed with us at the hospital, and the next day my mom and dad flew back from their vacation in Hawaii to be with us, too.

The doctors did dozens of tests on Kelty, trying to assess brain damage, but it soon became clear that there was no sign of activity. Kelty was not going to wake up; he was brain dead. I wouldn't accept it, though, wouldn't hear of it. Every time the doctors gave us an update, told us there was no hope, I said I knew Kelty was going to pull through. I would pray for him, will him to get better, just like I had done for Riley when she was a baby.

I sat by Kelty's bedside for hours. I held his hand, stroked his hair and his face, and whispered to him, "Kelts, you can't leave me. I need you. You are part of me. I can't imagine my life without you."

After two days, my dad gently took me aside. "You know, Ginny, Kelty's gone. The Kelty that we know is gone. You've got to let him go."

I argued with him. "How can you let someone go who is so young and so full of life, someone you love so much? How can you do that?"

"You just have to, Ginny," Dad said, a sadness in his eyes I had never seen before.

I knew deep in the pit of my stomach that he was right. Somehow, in the fog of grief and disbelief, I had to accept that my beloved Kelty was gone. The hospital counsellor, a lovely woman, sat me down and told me something about suicide that would bring me much comfort in the years ahead.

"Usually," she said, "people take their lives in the place where they feel they are most loved."

Kelty had hung himself in my office. He had moved a family photograph of the four of us from a bookshelf in the great room and onto the desk in the office, where he could see it.

I knew we had to let him go. We talked to the medical staff about how Kelty had been such a giving boy and how, if his life had to end, we wanted some good to come from that loss. We had never discussed it, as a family or between mother and son, but I felt intuitively that by donating his organs to those who needed them, Kelty would be giving the ultimate gift. Kerry agreed, and we signed the papers.

They took Kelty off life support on March 2, unplugging all the machines and removing all the tubes that had been keeping his body going. They moved him into a quiet room so that we could be with him, Kerry and Riley and me and his beloved nanny Imelda. We were the ones who loved him most, gathering in sorrow around his bedside to say goodbye.

It was so hard to kiss his cheek and turn away from him and finally walk toward the door, knowing that we would never see our son again; never hear his laugh or catch that twinkle in his eye; never feel his bear hug or the warm sweetness of his breath; never hear him say, as he always did: "Hey, Mom, hey, Dad, what do you think about this?"

A light in the firmament of our family had gone out. We had to keep that light burning, though, and so we decided right there in the hospital that we would fight back against this unforgiving monster that had taken our son's life and destroyed the lives of thousands of others. We vowed to start a foundation in his name. We didn't know yet what the foundation would look like or how it would work, but we were so sure about it that we decided to include a note in

Kelty's obituary suggesting that in lieu of flowers we would accept cheques for his new foundation. My friend Barb, once again so helpful, arranged to set up a bank account in Toronto and provide an address for donations. In the face of such unfathomable loss, we were choosing hope.

That night, we gathered as a family at a lovely restaurant in Vancouver's West End to celebrate Kelty. We did our best to get through it, but we were all in shock, floating through a nightmare from which there was no waking up. Things were made even more difficult when the hospital kept calling and asking us questions about Kelty, information they needed for the organ donation process. I could only hand the phone to Kerry. We would find out later that eight of his organs were used to help others.

The funeral was on March 8, a sunny spring day. Our Lady of the Mountains Catholic Church overflowed with family and friends, dozens upon dozens filing into the pews as James Taylor's sweet song "You've Got a Friend" filled the air. Kerry spoke tenderly of our dear son, of the joy and pride he had brought to our lives and to others. My brother Ted had written a song about Kelty called "He Was Taken," and he sang it to the congregation, a tender paean to a troubled boy that opened, "The demons came, they came to stay / We couldn't make them go away."

The heartbreaking and meaningful tributes from so many brought me a kind of peace. I was grateful to be surrounded by love, by people who mattered to me, like my brothers and sisters, my parents, and my best friend, Clare, who had come out from Winnipeg. Tears and laughter accompanied the many stories and memories of our Kelty shared at the reception that followed. Suddenly, I couldn't bear to let Riley out of my sight.

Kerry and I had decided to share something very intimate about Kelty's death: the suicide note he had left behind. Several days before, when the police came to the house to wrap up the details of their investigation, they had returned the note to us. We had made photocopies, then tied each one with a yellow ribbon, and we handed them out as people left the funeral. We released yellow balloons into the air and watched as two glorious white snow geese flew by. From the beginning, we wanted to be open about the deadly disease of depression, which is so often swept under the carpet and stigmatized by society.

Kelty's note, so achingly mature, said it better than we ever could: "Don't worry; I will be watching you from the heavens above. Heaven is a better place than earth. I love you Mom, Dad, Rye and family and friends. No research will understand the depression. The depression was in my mind. Peace and I love you all. God Bless. Kelty."

(4)

....

The Kelty Patrick Dennehy Foundation

....

IN THE WEEKS after Kelty's funeral, Kerry and Riley and I struggled to carry on. Loss and grief clouded every moment. People told us that time would help, that the pain would gradually ease, the sun would come out again, and the bad memories would fade while the good memories grew stronger. Intellectually, I knew that was probably true. But it was hard for me to see beyond the present, the next agonizing minute in front of me.

It was hard, too, for those around us. Many people weren't sure what to do or say when they ran into me at the grocery store or out walking. Should they hug me, offer condolences, or refrain from saying anything for fear that I would fall apart? But everyone was so kind. People brought us food and offered to help with anything we needed. Family and friends descended on the house, gathering in a tight protective net as we woke up every day to face life without Kelty.

My side of the family was also dealing with another loss: my brother Rob, who had battled his own demons and illnesses, had died during the week of Kelty's funeral. I was too numbed by grief over Kelty to be much of a comfort to my mom and dad, but it must have been terrible for them to lose a son and grandson within days of each other.

A group of my Whistler girlfriends would arrive at my front door every morning. I had taken time off work on short-term disability, but my friends didn't think it was healthy for me to be inside the house all day, so they would arrive in a pack of chattering friendliness, tell me to get dressed and put on my walking shoes, and then off we'd go for a brisk jaunt around the golf course or the lake. Jane Clifford was among them; she was the mother of Tom, who was dating Riley at the time, and she was very supportive of Riley in the early days after her brother's death. Others were the moms of Kelty's friends. Some of them I didn't know that well because I was always working or away on business. But their support was amazing, and it was a natural therapy that helped me heal.

Some days, though, I just couldn't get out of bed. It was late spring, and all of Kelty's friends were graduating and getting ready for university. Although I wanted the other mothers to be excited about their children heading off to school and I understood why they wanted to talk about it, sometimes I just couldn't listen. Kelty would never go to Bishop's, would never become the lawyer he had dreamed of being. The pain of that reality was like a stab in my heart. I came to know my limits when the social conversation turned to children and the future, and I would respectfully absent myself.

Kerry found comfort in his religion, and he began going to church again. I was glad for that. I went with him sometimes but stopped when I could no longer listen to the priest talking about God being good. I didn't believe that a good God would have taken Kelty, treated our family so harshly.

The grieving process was much different for Riley. She was only fifteen, and as much as we tried to console her, there was no explaining Kelty's death in a way that made sense. Riley had always been a quiet girl, the kind who would sit back and consider her choices before making a move. Now she retreated even farther into herself. She wouldn't talk to us about Kelty's death, and she rejected outright our urging that she see a counsellor. I was grateful that she spent a lot of time with her best friend, Britt. I knew they talked about everything, and that made me feel better. But I was still worried. Worried about how she was doing, and worried that something would happen to her, too.

Shortly after the funeral, Kerry and I had taken Riley on a trip to Hawaii to get her away from the raw reality of her brother's death. We rented a one-bedroom condo in Kauai and spent a week there. It was so gorgeous and calming. Riley and I slept together because we wanted to be close, while Kerry slept on the couch. I was finally able to get some rest, even though I couldn't stop thinking about Kelty. The first night there I had a dream that was so crystal clear I can still recall every detail. I was sitting at a bar and Kelty was standing at the other end, looking strapping and handsome and charming. He said, "Mom, I'm okay. Don't worry. I'm okay." It was so real that I felt like I could reach out and touch him. But when I opened my eyes, he was gone.

Hawaii, with its sunshine and fresh air, so far away from home, was good for us. We spent a lot of time on the beach and in the water. Even so, Kelty's death hung in the air like a heavy curtain, and we had to take things a day at a time.

On one foray into a jewellery store, I bought whale tail necklaces for all my girlfriends to thank them for their support. Riley and I each bought a cross on a chain, our way of remembering Kelty.

One afternoon, Riley and I were sitting on the verandah outside our condo while Kerry snorkelled just offshore. I could hear the people next door talking about spotting sharks in the water nearby, and suddenly I was panic-stricken. All I could think was, "Oh, my God. I just lost my son, and now my husband is going to be eaten by a shark." It was as if there would be no more in-between for me—I had experienced the worst and now, in a way, I expected it.

Once we got home, I wanted to know, needed to know, where Riley was all the time. If she wanted anything, I bought it for her. Expensive jeans? Sure. A new jacket? Okay. Her father had always watched our family finances carefully, and while Riley was walking around in $150 jeans, Kerry would be sporting a pair of $30 Levis from the Army & Navy. Riley and I chuckled about it, waiting outside in the car while Kerry was in a store checking out the bargains.

Riley had been something of a tomboy growing up, with short hair and baggy clothes, but as a teenager she was increasingly conscious of how she looked. She liked nice clothes, and she even modelled briefly—one job had her bungee jumping with a "groom" in a mock wedding ceremony. She was constantly fussing with the colour of her hair, lightening up her natural ash blond and going crazy with the streaks. She wore coloured contacts to make her eyes bluer. It was hard on my bank balance, and I know now that my indulgence with material things was part of my guilt and pain over losing Kelty. Riley wasn't the best driver, and she managed to smash my car up a few times, which didn't make Kerry happy. He thought I was spoiling her too much. But I just didn't care.

After Hawaii, I had to face Kelty's room. And not just his room, with his clothes and all his things, but the little pieces of him that could be found in every corner of the house: photographs, notes, his favourite cereal, the chair he always sat in, his hockey gear and snowboard, the movies on the shelf that he would make us watch over and over, the CDs that used to blare from the sports room. Several weeks after he died, Notre Dame shipped his clothing and school items to us. When I opened the first box and found a pile of Valentine's Day cards that he had received from his school friends, I closed it right back up and didn't open it again for the next ten years.

The Notre Dame Grade 12 Spirit of Strength annual, dedicated to "the memory of our dear friend, roommate, teammate and fellow Hound Kelty," was hard to thumb through, with the photographs of his classmates and friends and the snapshot of a sharply dressed Kelty and his friends at the winter formal, all of them so full of promise. Noah, one of his best friends at Notre Dame, wrote a graduation blurb that said: "Kelty, you were and are the best friend I'll ever have. I'll cherish your memory forever. Being around you made me happy to be alive and the impact you've had on my life is immeasurable. Peace out, Dr. D." Neal, his other good Notre Dame buddy, was no less heartfelt: "Kelty was a person who came and left, but will never be truly gone. He will live forever in my mind and in my heart and that is where I will always hold his memory closest."

I couldn't leave Kelty's room like it was, as if he might just wander in and throw his jacket on the bed. I put some of his clothes in the bottom drawer of the dresser, though

I didn't touch the closet. I moved some of the furniture, as well, but I didn't want to change the room too much; it was the place I would go to be close to Kelty, sitting on the window seat and feeling his presence. I kept some of his school essays on religion, and reading them helped me to understand that Catholicism had been his friend toward the end.

One day I decided to commission a family portrait by Kelowna artist Rod Charlesworth, whose work I had long admired. His paintings were colourful and happy. I provided photos of Kelty in his Notre Dame Hounds jersey, Kerry in his Hollyburn senior men's hockey jersey, and Riley in her Whistler Winterhawks hockey jersey, saying simply that these were the three most significant people in my life. The finished painting, which Rod titled *He Shoots, He Scores*, depicts Kerry and Kelty exuberantly playing hockey on a frozen pond. Kelty, clad in his red Notre Dame uniform, is scoring a goal against Kerry, who is kneeling in an attempt to stop the shot in his green and white hockey gear. In the background are snow-covered cottages, and at the pond's edge a woman in a purple coat is watching, a small dog at her side. In the painting's foreground, on the opposite edge of the pond, a jersey-clad child is brandishing her own hockey stick. I hadn't mentioned to Rod that I wanted to be in the painting, but there we all were, the four of us together again. The portrait was better than I could have dreamed, and today it is the first thing you see when you walk into Kelty's room. Later, we would turn it into a note card used by the Kelty Patrick Dennehy Foundation.

That June, I fulfilled a promise I had made to my son: I went to his graduation. Kelty had always teased that I'd be away on a business trip at graduation time. We would laugh about it, and I would assure him that I'd be in the front row, wearing a new outfit.

So there I was, with Kerry and Riley by my side, in a brand new outfit, sitting in the front row at Notre Dame College as Kelty's classmates received their diplomas. There was a photo tribute to Kelty, and that seemed to bring him alive again, if only for a few hours. The school welcomed us with open arms, and at the celebratory dinner we were seated at the headmaster's table. Before we left, I gave each of his friends a photograph of Kelty wearing his Hounds jersey.

I learned in those first few months after Kelty's death that the grieving process was just that: a process. We all handle profound loss differently, and there is no right way to grieve, despite what some experts say. Sometimes I would be sad while Kerry was fine. Other times I would be feeling okay, but Kerry was blue. We talked constantly about what had happened and how we felt. We didn't blame each other; it was more that each of us blamed ourselves, me for going away, Kerry for going skiing. We know now that it was normal to feel that way. And we weren't angry—at Kelty or anyone else. We could not have loved our son any more than we did, and Kelty had known that, too. However, the chemicals that alter our brains are more powerful than all the love in the world, and Kelty couldn't help what had happened to him. Now Kerry and I needed to find a way to go on, for Kelty, for each other, and for our daughter.

I admit that at first I didn't want to. I wanted to die so that I would be with Kelty. I thought Kerry and Riley would be better off without me, a wife and mother so immersed in grief that nothing else seemed to register. I didn't understand at the time that this was part of my own depression. Like Kelty, I couldn't see past it. One day I went out to our garage, determined to get in the car, turn on the exhaust, and kill myself. But as I sat there in the front seat, it was as if a light switched on in my head. I knew I couldn't do it, that it wouldn't be fair to Kerry and Riley, to our family and friends. I had to dig deeper, try harder to cope, be stronger for them. I got out of the car and went back in the house.

When I talked to Kerry about it afterward, he was devastated and scared. After he confided in Sue Dowler, Kelty's godmother, Sue insisted that I come to stay with her in California. She took me to a counsellor, and she and I went shopping and ate too many French fries while we talked and talked. It was good for me.

Once I got home, Kerry and I decided to renovate the kids' area downstairs. We installed an en suite bathroom in Riley's room, and she loved having a bathroom of her own, but it must have been hard living down there without her brother. She had never liked being alone. When we first moved into the house, she had hated being downstairs, even with Kelty nearby. She'd come up into our room at night, carrying her favourite blankets, and make a little bed on the floor of our room so that she could fall asleep close to us. She'd eventually grown out of it and come to appreciate her own space. Now, though, she had to walk by Kelty's quiet, empty room every day.

About six months after Kelty's death, and just after the 9/11 terrorist attacks in New York City, I had to go to Vancouver for a psychiatric assessment related to my disability claim. I had been taking antidepressants, which were helping, but the doctor the company made me see started asking questions clearly designed to make me feel guilty about losing my son, as if it was my fault. I was a wreck afterward and could hardly drive home. I decided to go off the antidepressants because I'd heard that when you stop taking them, you just go through the grieving process all over again. I couldn't face that. My family doctor agreed and began weaning me off them.

Kelty had been cremated, his treasured Todeye teddy bear beside him, and we divided the ashes among three meaningful locations. We scattered some on the golf course greenery right in front of our house. At Lake George, a fishing camp in northern Manitoba where Kerry and the kids often spent time in the summer, we took a boat out into the middle of the lake and let some of Kelty's ashes drift away gently on the wind. It seemed natural that he was now part of a place he had so loved. And then, on a fall day, we buried the rest of his ashes in a small urn in our family plot at the Whistler cemetery, where the air is still but for the chirping of birds and moss covers the trees. Afterward, Kerry had a surprise for Riley and me: he had arranged for us to go on an ATV tour of Whistler Mountain. It was absolutely the best way to celebrate Kelty. One of our most precious photographs was taken that day, the three of us wearing bright yellow rain slickers, our faces sunburned, wheeling free through the Whistler wilderness. We would have the picture made into a Christmas card that we sent out that year, with an inscription that read in part: We each, at our own pace, continue our journey of healing. It is the support and love from all of you, our family and friends, that have helped so much on this continued journey. Kerry, Riley and I want to wish you and your families a very Merry Christmas and may the year 2002 be one of peace and happiness for all.

THERE ARE MANY groups for those who want to talk about how suicide has affected their lives, many places to go for parents looking for others who understand what they're going through. That kind of informal therapy helps many people, but I knew it wasn't for me. I didn't want to share my feelings about Kelty's suicide; I wanted to discuss the reasons for it. I wanted to talk about why suicide happens, why no one thinks of depression as a disease, why there isn't more general knowledge about indicators and prevention. I wanted everyone to know that depression is the killer you can't see, that it has no boundaries. It's about falling into an invisible abyss from which there seems no way out.

From the beginning, the goal of the Kelty Patrick Dennehy Foundation was to raise money to help prevent depression-related suicide among youth. Beyond that, we didn't really know what things would look like. Don Jordan, a lawyer who is one of our good friends, guided us through legalities such as registering the foundation as a non-profit charity. We needed a board and members to sit on it, so Kerry and I convened a meeting that summer in the family cabin in Winnipeg, with a big group of friends and family who knew we were on a mission and wanted to help. It was an impressive bunch, representing years of business expertise and ideas about the work ahead. We decided on a mandate and fine-tuned our mission statement: the Kelty Patrick Dennehy Foundation would raise funds for care, education, and research into youth depression-related suicide.

It was an ambitious credo, and the discussion went on for hours. We decided to form specific committees, with people volunteering to work on areas relevant to their own experience—fundraising, marketing, and so on—but the truth is we were all rather naïve about the process. We decided that Kerry would be president and I would be secretary. Others were board members with specific duties, such as treasurer and directors. We also decided to start an offshoot we called the Kelty Circle. That would allow people who wanted to give more financially a way to do that. To become a guardian of the Kelty Circle, members would commit $10,000 a year for three years. Kerry and I became members, as did many of our friends and associates. Over the years, the Kelty Circle would become an integral part of the foundation's endowment funding.

It was August 2001. The Kelty Patrick Dennehy Foundation was up and running, though we had no idea how successful it would become.

Soon after Kerry and I returned to Whistler, a friend who had heard about our fledgling foundation gave us a call. Rod Cochrane was the general manager at Nicklaus North Golf Course. Kelty had worked at the golf course, so Rod knew us and he knew about Kelty. He suggested we hold a fundraising golf tournament for the foundation in September 2002. He had already given it a lot of thought. It would be a quality weekend event, he said, with a banquet, golfing, first-class auctions, and plenty of marketing to get the word out. We agreed that it was a great idea, so we got to work, putting together a golf committee and assigning everyone jobs. It seemed that everyone we knew got on board. Over the next eleven months, local businesses donated goods and services for the silent and live auctions—wonderful things like trips to Mexico and Maui and Bermuda, as well as golf clubs, art, jewellery, and electronics.

We dubbed the tournament Drive Fore Life. In our inaugural year, we attracted three hundred people, each of whom paid $100 for dinner or $500 if they were signed up for the whole weekend. Dozens of locals were there, as were friends and family from Vancouver and Winnipeg. It was a rousing success. We raised $125,000, which we immediately invested to start a foundation nest egg we hoped would grow over the years.

We shifted the tournament to the Fairmont Chateau Whistler Golf Club the second year, following Rod, who had changed jobs. Over the years to come, we worked with a number of general managers at the Fairmont, and each was wonderful. Drive Fore Life, which we also called A Weekend to Remember, would always begin with a Friday night blowout at Buffalo Bills in Whistler, with live music by Don Jordan's band, a group of rocking baby boomers who called themselves Fabulous George and the Zodiacs. Saturday was the dinner, a full-dress affair that included a fantastic meal, an emotional tribute to Kelty, lots of lively music, and several speeches. Kerry usually said a few words, and we made sure to acknowledge those whose work was helping the foundation to spread the word about depression and suicide. One year, Ali Milner, a talented young Whistler singer who would appear in 2011 on the CBC reality show *Cover Me Canada*, wrote a song for Kelty titled "My Beautiful Boy" and sang it at the dinner. The weekend wrapped up on Sunday with a rousing round of golf. Kelty's friends were recruited as caddies for each foursome on the course, and Riley and her friends signed on as volunteers. All of them wore bright red Kelty Patrick Dennehy Foundation bibs. It became a huge annual event for Whistler.

The foundation's first year was a busy one. Several local mental health organizations wanted to talk to us about what they did and how they might approach us for specific funding. We were invited to lots of events, giving speech after speech about our story and outlining the goals and aspirations of the foundation. Kerry took the lead on the public speaking at first.

In 2002, I met Sue Carruthers, the new CEO of the B.C. Children's Hospital Foundation. The hospital was raising money for a new mental health centre to be opened in the renovated four-storey Jean Matheson Memorial Pavilion. When she and some of her employees took our board on a tour of the hospital's existing mental health facilities, we were shocked. There were programs spread over different floors of the hospital instead of one dedicated area where people could find the treatment and resources they needed. It was pathetic. There were even offices in broom closets. This new mental health centre was badly needed.

Our family already had a strong connection to Children's, having spent so many days there when Riley was a child. As far as I was concerned, they had saved Riley's life on our first visit. Now we had a chance to give back for Kelty and for our daughter, who had grown into a healthy, vibrant young woman.

Kerry agreed our foundation should become involved in the new mental health centre, but it was a bit of a challenge to get everyone on the board onside. The problem was that the new centre wasn't focussed just on depression—it would also be addressing issues such as eating disorders, attention deficit and hyperactivity disorder, and schizophrenia. Some board members felt that by joining forces with such a wide-ranging initiative, our cause would be diluted. However, I argued that depression is often the common denominator in mental illnesses, especially in adolescents. The board finally agreed, and suddenly our little foundation had entered the big time.

We had high hopes that the new mental health centre might be named after Kelty, but we soon discovered that naming rights of that magnitude would require a $10-million donation. That was a bit rich for our foundation's means. We also learned that the centre needed a significant private donation to get things started, and that quickly became our goal. We committed to raising $1 million, and over the next four years we did that through the Kelty Circle and the golf tournaments. When we handed over the cheque, the hospital foundation told us our donation was the turning point in the provincial government's decision to provide funding for the centre. The Kelty Patrick Dennehy Foundation would go on to be the top private contributor to the B.C. Children's Hospital mental health centre.

The hospital's official fundraising campaign was launched in October 2004, and by spring 2005 construction on the building had begun. The centre opened officially on January 29, 2007, nearly six years after we had lost Kelty. There was a wing dedicated to our son, with a plaque at the entrance and his photograph. On the day of the dedication, we toured the wing, and then Kerry and Riley and I had our picture taken at the site. We were there for the formal ceremonies, too, gladly sitting through speeches by dignitaries, hospital officials, and politicians. They had asked me to speak, too, and I did, about how important it is to talk openly about mental illness. It was a proud moment for the foundation and for our family.

It was during this hectic time that Kerry and I met Lloyd and Heather Craig. Lloyd was then CEO of the Surrey Credit Union, and he and Heather had lost their twenty-five-year-old son Gavin to suicide in the fall of 2001. When the four of us got together for lunch in Whistler one day, the Craigs told us they were working with the University of British Columbia medical faculty and the VGH Foundation to raise $4.5 million to endow a mental health chair for the university. The plan was to hire an international expert who would conduct research and raise the profile of depression and the need for detection and treatment. They asked us to join their undertaking.

Kerry and I liked the idea, as did the rest of the board. However, we were adamant that whoever was hired be not only renowned and credible in the field of mental health but also personable. He or she had to be someone approachable who could get the message out to both adults and young people, especially the vulnerable "lost" group between the ages of nineteen and twenty-five.

Lloyd was an indefatigable proponent of the new position, and he engaged credit union members all over the province, asking them to pledge a mere $1 each to the cause. One million of them did. He raised another $800,000 through charity golf tournaments, and when our foundation donated $500,000, the proposal became a reality. In 2005, psychiatrist Dr. Allan Young was recruited from a university in Britain to become the first chair of UBC's new B.C. Credit Union Centre of Excellence for Depression Research and Care. The provincial government under then premier Gordon Campbell had matched the $2.5 million raised by our foundation and the Craigs' efforts, resulting in $5 million for the UBC program. (Campbell had also been touched by the disease of depression—his father, Charles, had committed suicide in 1961.)

Allan Young was a wonderful catch, a celebrated pioneer in the use of brain imaging as a way to study mental illness. He was not shy about speaking on "the monster disease" at events all over Greater Vancouver, reminding the media that it was important to dispel the myths and report the facts about depression. He was learned, amiable, and a father himself. We were especially pleased with his public stance on depression. "It's about promoting a shift in culture. Of holding stigma up to the light and letting it be seen for what it is—nothing less than prejudice," Allan told the *Vancouver Sun*. Not long after, our foundation pledged another $500,000 to the UBC project so that Allan and his team could conduct a multi-year study into the relationship between age and vulnerability to mood disorders, adolescent depression, and suicide.

One of my duties from the beginning was to be the face of the foundation. I'd never had a hard time talking—people always said that Kelty got his love of the spotlight from me—but standing up in front of strangers to talk about such personal events was nerve-wracking at first. I gave one of my first speeches several months after Kelty died to the Young Presidents' Organization, which was holding an event on giving back. The YPO is an international organization of CEOs under the age of forty-five who share a mission of gaining leadership values through education and the exchange of ideas. Kerry and I were happy to talk about Kelty and our decision to start the foundation. Kerry started off, and he was his usual confident and engaging self. Then I got up and emotionally told the audience what it was like to go through Kelty's illness and suicide. At one point, a woman stood up and said, "My brother took his life, and I've never talked about it." Several other people in the room followed suit. Suddenly, we were lifting the cloak of secrecy that has so long shrouded the topic of depression. As hard as it was to hear their stories and relive ours—something that continues to be difficult to this day, every time we appear at an event or give a speech—we knew that we were making a difference.

I was invited to speak at the 2002 B.C. Children's Hospital Crystal Ball, the hospital foundation's annual fundraiser at the Four Seasons Hotel in Vancouver. It was a lavish, well-attended event, and I was nervous. But I knew by that point that we had committed the foundation to raising money for the new mental health centre, and I needed to get our message out. I spoke at the same event in 2004.

Riley was involved from the time the foundation began its work. She came along to most of the events, to the dinners and out on the golf course, but mostly stayed in the background, occasionally posing for photographs but never speaking in public. It was wonderful to have her there, but I would learn that even though she never talked about it, it was hard to see all of us so focussed on the brother she had lost.

By the time we were forced to cancel the golf tournament in 2008 because of shifting economic realities, we were proud to have raised an astonishing $1.5 million from the tournament revenue alone, testimony not only to the hard work of our board and volunteers but also to the generosity of the community. The board got together to decide on our next move. We held two Dance Fore Life events at Bar None in Vancouver, based on the successful fundraisers we'd previously held at Buffalo Bills in Whistler. We raised $7,000 or so and had a great time. The Kelty Circle, along with assorted donations and other small fundraisers, kept the foundation and its endowment going strong.

BELOW Ginny (*front row left*) and her sister
Catherine were flower girls at the wedding of
their Auntie Rae and Uncle Bob (*back row right*)
in 1956. Their aunt and uncle adopted Ginny
and her three siblings after the death of their
parents, E.P. Wood and Barbara Wood (*shown
here top left*).

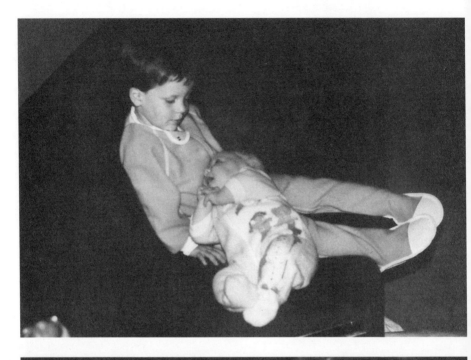

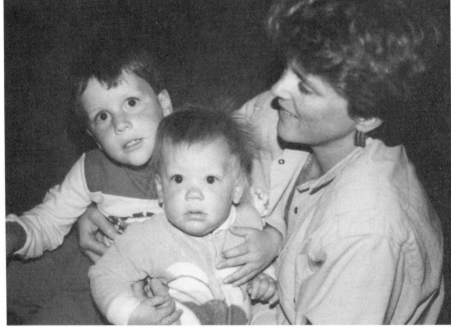

TOP LEFT Kelty and Riley with their Uncle Ted Spear, who years later wrote and sang a song for each of them at their funeral services.

BOTTOM LEFT Kelty, Riley, and Kerry enjoying a snack at the base of the mountain in Whistler.

BELOW Kelty and Riley sharing a laugh, 1990.

BELOW Kelty's Hadden House preschool picture, 1987.

TOP RIGHT Ginny and the kids on the deck of their family home in West Vancouver, early 1990s.

BOTTOM RIGHT When she was small, Riley loved swinging more than anything else.

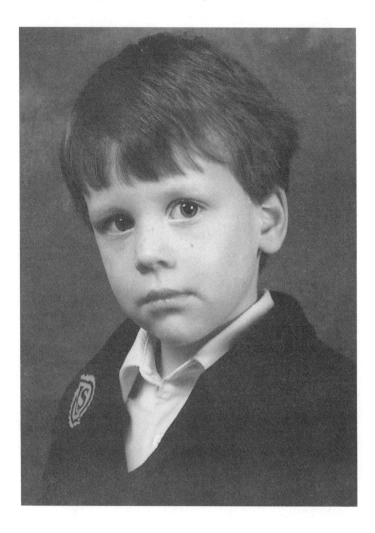

TOP LEFT Best friends Kelty and Riley in Florida, winter 1998.

BOTTOM LEFT The whole family, along with Kelly the dog, poses on the windy West Vancouver seawall.

BELOW Kelty caddying at the Skins game at Nicklaus North in 1996 with pro golf superstar Nick Faldo. *Bob Huxtable, Huxtable Productions*

BELOW   Riley (*right*) and her best friend, Britt Gibbons, ready for their Grade 6 graduation.

TOP RIGHT   Kelty in his Notre Dame Hounds uniform, 2000.

BOTTOM RIGHT   Riley with her mom and dad on February 14, 2001, just before the Valentine's Day dance at Whistler Secondary School.

BELOW ATVing on Whistler Mountain after burying Kelty's ashes at the Whistler cemetery.

TOP RIGHT The Dennehy clan at Lake George, Manitoba, after spreading some of Kelty's ashes on the water. Kelty had spent many wonderful times at the lake with his dad and his friends.

BOTTOM RIGHT Kelty and her dad, Kerry, on a kayak trip near Zeballos on Vancouver Island.

LEFT Riley playing hockey at the B.C. Winter Games, 2002.

BELOW Riley and her grandfather, Papa, at the Drive Fore Life dinner at the Fairmont Chateau Whistler, 2006.

BELOW Riley and her best friend, Britt, in their early twenties.

RIGHT Riley bungee jumping for a modelling assignment, 2007. *Photograph courtesy Whistler Bungee*

(5)

·················

Riley

·················

THE MONTHS AFTER Kelty died had been rough for Riley. In June 2001, she came home from school and told us that she wanted to go to the Notre Dame summer hockey school with her cousin from Calgary. Riley was a good player, had been from the start, and she played forward for the Whistler Winterhawks. Hockey was a rough sport for someone with her history of illnesses, but Rye worked hard at whatever she did. After Kelty died, she changed the number on her jersey to seventeen to honour him. Her Notre Dame request surprised us, but we agreed, and off she went.

She loved the hockey school, and when she came back she informed us that she wanted to go to Notre Dame that fall for Grade 10. I was screaming inside. It was as if she was following her brother's lead, and I couldn't face it. I was afraid to let her go, worried about feeling even more empty than I already did. But Kerry and I talked about it, and I relented. Even though she didn't articulate it, I knew it was Riley's way of escaping the grief and the too-visible memories of Kelty.

Toward the end of August, I flew with Riley to Notre Dame. Just like I had done for Kelty, I got her settled into her dorm room. Letting my other baby go was harder than I could have imagined. I had a lump in my throat as I watched her walk around the campus; I was proud that she was maturing into a beautiful young woman but scared about what the future might hold.

Riley liked her new school, and in our frequent phone chats she seemed to be doing well, both in her studies and in her social life. Then, just before Thanksgiving, she called home in tears. A girl in her dorm, a girl she knew from summer hockey camp, had committed suicide. Riley was devastated. She didn't want to stay at Notre Dame. We got her on the next flight out and picked her up at the airport the next day. I squeezed her so hard when I saw her that I'm sure she thought I would never let go.

Riley returned to Whistler Secondary, and at first it was as if she had never left. She was playing hockey again and snowboarding with her friends. But her grades started slipping, which was unusual. She seemed concerned mostly about things that didn't matter, like how she looked, and we couldn't get her to talk about what was bothering her.

That Christmas, our first without Kelty, Kerry decided we should rent out our house to tourists for New Year's Eve. We didn't want to go too far afield, so for fun we rented a cabin in the Whistler campground, and three of Kelty's friends from Notre Dame—Noah, Neal, and Hughie—joined us. We called them the Lost Boys. It was as if we had three Keltys staying with us, playing pool in the communal area, horsing around and bringing back to us, ever so briefly, a delightful piece of our son's life. Riley opted to spend the holidays with Britt and her family. We thought she couldn't bear to be around Kelty's friends.

We weren't surprised when Riley told us she didn't want to go back to Whistler Secondary for Grade 11. She wanted to go away to school, she said, somewhere far from our small town where everyone knew her. We tried to talk her out of it, but she was as persuasive as her brother had been. "Please, Mom," she said. "You let Kelty go away. Why can't I go away? I think it will be good for me. I need to get out of Whistler."

She was becoming lost in the shadow of her brother's death.

We checked out several private schools on Vancouver Island and settled on Shawnigan Lake in Cowichan Bay. We talked to the staff there about Riley and her background; they understood the challenges she was facing and said they would be happy to have her. In late August 2002, we were once again taking our child to a school far from home.

But Riley struggled at Shawnigan. She was always phoning us, and I was constantly heading to the ferry for visits to the school. I spent hours on the phone with her counsellors, trying to figure out what was going on and how to fix it. She didn't seem to feel good about anything. There was no hockey team at the school, so she played volleyball, but she wasn't good enough to make the first-string team. It eerily mirrored the disappointments Kelty had faced at Notre Dame, something that began to haunt me. It all haunted me: Riley's change in personality, her difficulties with academics, her anxiety and uneasiness. This couldn't be happening again, I told myself. It just couldn't. But the phone calls continued, and just before the end of the first term, I told her that we were done with Shawnigan. "You know what, Rye?" I said. "You're coming home. I know you think you need to be away, but you're just not ready." She didn't put up a fight, and she was back in Whistler the next day.

It wasn't long before I noticed how thin she was getting. Riley had always had an athletic build, and she was a careful eater, partly because of her allergies. Now she was clearly showing signs of bulimia, eating and purging so that she could control her weight. She brushed off my concerns, telling me I was overreacting. But it nagged at me, and one day the mother of one of Riley's buddies said, "You know, Ginny, I think Riley needs to see somebody." She recommended a Vancouver therapist who might be able to help. We insisted Riley see the therapist, and their relationship would last for several years. It seemed to help, though Riley—true to form—never said anything about those sessions to Kerry or me.

Back at Whistler Secondary for Grade 12, Riley fell right back into the social whirl. She worked part-time, as she always had, as a server at Earl's restaurant and then in a little sweater shop in Whistler village. She and the rest of her crowd spent their spare time up the mountain snowboarding or off the mountain drinking and getting into a little mischief. We weren't naïve parents, and we knew that Riley and her friends were probably smoking pot, too. We nursed her through the aftermath of more than one drinking incident, including the night she fell off the deck of a house still under construction and was rushed by ambulance to the Vancouver General Hospital spinal cord unit. She was lucky, ending up with only a few bruised ribs. "There must have been a guardian angel placing her on the ground," a nurse told us.

Another time, at a Christmas party while on a date with Britt's cousin Sam, Riley fell on top of a scalding woodstove, suffering second-degree burns on her arm. She was also caught driving under the influence by the Whistler police and had her licence suspended. It didn't stop her from drinking, but the impact on her mobility and her social life taught her a valuable lesson, and she vowed to never drive drunk again. Much to my consternation, Riley also smoked cigarettes. All teenagers think they're immortal, and Riley was no different. She didn't listen when I admonished her about smoking and reminded her that it was even more dangerous for someone with asthma.

Riley's last year at school was a rocky one. Because she had missed the requisite career prep course in Grade 11, she took the course online. I pretty much completed it for her, but I didn't feel guilty for one second. All I cared about was getting her through Grade 12, getting her to that graduation ceremony. When she made it, Kerry and I were both relieved and proud. Before we knew it, Riley was moving to Vancouver with her boyfriend, L.J., and signing up for arts courses at Langara College.

In October 2004, Kerry's brother Shaun died. He had been sick with cancer since before Kelty's death, but it was devastating for all of us. Shaun had always meant so much to us and to our kids. For Riley, the death of her uncle was just one more unbearable loss.

We were back from the funeral for what seemed like only a millisecond when Riley announced that she had broken up with L.J., was quitting Langara, and was heading to Los Angeles to visit her cousin Tegan, who was by then an established actress working in the movie business. She told us not to worry; she would bunk with Tegan, get an under-the-table job, and see how things went. I wasn't thrilled at the idea, but she was eighteen. We let her go.

She hadn't been there long before I got a frightening phone call. "Mom, I think I'm in trouble. I need help with this eating thing, because I can't control it on my own." I was terrified, but I was happy that Riley was reaching out. I immediately went into Mom mode, telling her to get on the next plane and come right back home. Before I could finish the sentence, she shut me down. "No, Mom, I need to do this on my own."

Worried, I immediately flew to Los Angeles as soon as I could. Riley was noticeably thinner. I got on the phone to her therapist back in Vancouver, and we started working on getting Riley into a facility that could help her. The Sierra Tucson treatment centre in Tucson, Arizona, instructed us to get a raft of tests done and send them the results. For the next few days, the emails flew back and forth.

Riley and I finally drove to Tucson for interviews, and we waited back at our hotel for a decision. Finally, the centre phoned to say they'd take her. It would cost $50,000 for the month or so she'd be there, but I didn't care. The centre asked that I stay in town for a week, having no contact with Riley, so that they could ensure that she was stable enough to undertake the program. They assured me they would call me regularly at the hotel to keep me updated, but I couldn't shake the feeling that I had abandoned her. It was a feeling I was starting to hate. I had felt it when my Grams died, then when Kelty died, and now here I was again, abandoning someone I loved. But at last the centre said Riley was okay and I could go home.

Three weeks into the program, Kerry and I flew to Tucson for parent week. We checked into a hotel for five days and began attending counselling sessions at the facility, some with just the three of us, others in group settings. It was gruelling to see our daughter so vulnerable and hear her talk about everything that was wrong with her life. At one

of the sessions, Riley focussed on her issues with us, mostly
with me. She said her eating disorder was my fault because
I always seemed to be on a diet and was never happy with
the way I looked.

Just as hurtful was Riley's revelation in another ses-
sion that I was devoting so much time to the Kelty Patrick
Dennehy Foundation that she felt neglected. "You care
more about a dead person than a live one," she accused. It
stunned me. I knew she needed to get these feelings off her
chest if she was going to deal with them, but it broke my
heart to hear her say such things. I had immersed myself in
the foundation as my way of making something meaningful out of Kelty's death, but my main concern had always
been Riley. I cared more about her than anything, and it was
hard to hear she didn't understand that. She had less criti-
cism for her father, but it didn't matter. Through it all, Kerry
and I simply sat and listened. This was Riley's way of dealing with her demons, and if she needed to place the blame
on our shoulders, so be it.

The staff at the centre told us that when Riley had finished her treatment to their satisfaction, she would be
moved to a halfway house to help her integrate back into
the community. They warned us that we should not be surprised if she replaced the bulimia with another addiction,
drugs or drinking or anything else that allowed her to be
in control and push away her pain. Riley refused to go to a
halfway house, though, insisting she could come home and
get on with her life. Kerry and I had returned to Whistler by
then, but I flew back to Tucson and took her to visit the recommended halfway houses, hoping she might change her
mind. But she'd had enough, and part of me could understand that. Since Kelty's death, I had been inundated with

advice, much of it in the form of books about the grieving process. But you can only take in so much. I think she was sick of all the analysis.

Riley came home, and she never had a problem with bulimia after that. But soon she was off on another track, wanting to join Tegan and Cath's son Jesse in the movie business. To do that, she said, she needed to go to Vancouver Film School. We enrolled her for the year-long program, starting in the spring of 2006.

She loved film school and immersed herself in her film production classes. She met a new set of friends, talented and committed young people who seemed to have a good sense of what they wanted out of life. But she was twenty and living in downtown Vancouver, where there were parties around every corner. She graduated from vfs in March 2007—her final project was an interview with the owners of the Kearney funeral home, a family dynasty. When she had no luck finding work, she moved back to Whistler again.

Kerry and I had the sense that our daughter was still feeling lost. And once again, she reached out for help. This time, her drinking was out of control. Alcohol would change her from a bright, vibrant girl to a babbling rag doll. It was as if she was allergic to it; even one glass of wine would set her off. She was never a mean drunk or an angry one. Instead, alcohol seemed to shut her down.

That Riley recognized this, and admitted she needed to do something about it, made me proud of her. And again, despite how difficult it was, I felt some relief. She was still seeing Pat, her therapist, and that seemed to help, but Riley never told me what they talked about. It was all part of her trying to find her own way, to find her path. It worried me, but I was her mother, and it was my job to do everything I could to get her where she needed to go to have a healthy, happy life.

I got her into Cedars, a rehab centre on Vancouver Island, where she stayed for a month. I went on weekends to visit her and once took Britt and Colleen. She was doing well and made some good friends. But, as before, the experts at the facility warned us not to expect miracles. Riley might well substitute one addiction for another.

I'd been back at work since January 2002, slipping into my old job and grateful for the kindness of my IBM co-workers and customers after Kelty's death. In the fall of 2008, I had just returned from a holiday in Mexico with some girl-friends when I got a call from my boss, asking me to meet him in the company's Vancouver office. After twenty-eight years, at the age of fifty-six, I was getting downsized. I walked away with a severance check and a crushed ego. It wasn't long before I realized it was a good thing, though. Now I was free to focus on Riley and on Kelty's foundation, no longer tied to the travelling, early-morning phone calls, and late-night faxes that went with the job.

Riley had finished her stint at Cedars and was back living with us and working at Earl's. She had decided to get a tattoo in honour of her brother—his initials, KPD. Although I wasn't keen on the idea, I understood why she wanted to memorialize her brother, to have him with her always. The tattoo was on her inner arm, and sometimes customers at the restaurant would comment on it. That made her uncomfortable, because she didn't like talking about Kelty with strangers. Britt and Rye had also gotten matching tattoos on their backs: two parallel lines that signified they were on the same path together through life, side by side, and that their future together was eternal. She was still tight with

Britt, who had been going through her own issues. Britt was gay, and although that was no secret, there was often drama involving her girlfriends. I once asked Riley if there was anything beyond friendship between them, and she was horrified. "Mom, no way. It's not like that at all." They both felt like outsiders in their own way, and theirs was one of those unbreakable bonds.

Riley was also helping us with the foundation, going to dedications and participating in the annual fundraising golf tournaments we held in Whistler. We could see that she was working hard to turn her life around.

Most importantly, she had discovered yoga. It gave her the discipline she craved, and it became her lifesaver. Soon she was immersed not just in yoga's stoic athleticism and the community of its practitioners but in the tranquil spiritual fold of Buddhism. Britt's aunt Dee Dee was a yoga teacher, and she had a great influence on Riley, becoming a friend and confidante.

Before long, Riley was asking us if she could take a yoga training course in Whistler. It was a month-long, two-hundred-hour course designed to teach every aspect of the yoga lifestyle, from nutrition to the types of yoga practised around the world. We had put money aside for her post-secondary education, but film school and her other pursuits had caused it to dwindle. We told her yes, but said she needed to be sure about it because the money we had for that purpose was finite.

She took the class and blossomed. Our daughter had found her calling.

Riley began researching courses that would further her studies and help her achieve her goal of becoming a yoga teacher. One of the best, she told us, was a three-month master course on a little island off the coast of Thailand. I could tell she was serious about it. "Okay, Rye," I said. "If you really want to do this, that's fine. But you have to understand that you can't come back from this yoga course and then say you want to go to university, because the money we saved for your education will be gone."

She didn't hesitate. "No, Mom, I have never felt so good about myself, and this is what I want to do."

Riley had not travelled much, and when she did it was usually on family vacations. This time she would be going halfway around the world on her own. My worry meter was registering off the chart, but I knew I had to let my girl spread her wings.

It was June 2008. My dad had been very sick with heart problems, and I ended up heading back to Winnipeg to see him on the same day that Riley was flying to Phuket. She had planned a stop on the Thai resort island for a few days to get acclimatized; she would be staying at a hotel owned by the brother of one of our neighbours, Peter Fu. We both had early-morning flights out of Vancouver, so Kerry came with us and the three of us stayed overnight at the airport hotel.

The next morning, I offered to walk Riley to her gate. She looked at me and smiled. "Mom, it's okay. I love you, but I've got to do this on my own."

She was telling me it was a step into her future that she needed to take without me. I gave her a big hug, squeezed her as tight as I could, and told her to call the minute she landed. I watched as she walked toward the gate, so beautiful, so full of life, her dad by her side.

I had no way of knowing it was the last time I would see her.

I was in Winnipeg the next day when I got a call from Peter Fu. He didn't want me to worry, he said, but Riley had been playing in the waves in the ocean on Phuket and had separated her shoulder. I wasn't too upset. She'd always had a wonky shoulder—it had separated before—and Peter assured me that his brother had made sure she'd gone to a doctor and the problem was fixed. The next day, Riley called to reassure me that all was well.

She started the yoga program with her arm in a sling. But the centre wasn't quite as advertised, it turned out, and Riley complained to me over the phone that the facilities weren't up to snuff. I reminded her that she was in Thailand, not Paris, and that she needed to revel in the moment, concentrating on what she had gone there to do. She laughed and agreed.

We emailed back and forth regularly over the next few months. Riley regaled me with all her adventures. She was having fun with the other students, amazing people from places like Berlin and Australia. On her time off she was seeing the sights on a scooter and getting to know the Thai people and their colourful culture.

During one of my Skype chats with her in Chiang Mai, where she went after she finished the master course, Riley told me she was going to stay a bit longer to research courses in Thai massage. She felt she needed to expand her knowledge if she was going to open her own studio in Whistler, which had become her dream.

We arranged to talk again a few days later to discuss which school she had chosen. I was happy for her. The day before she had sent me an email saying how content she was and how excited about the future. She'd ended by saying how much she loved me:

pps—thank you so much for everything, you are an amazing mom/person! and that is an understatement, words don't describe how incredible you are… This experience has really opened up my eyes to the way some people live. I feel very grateful to be who I am, and the people that I have been surrounded by my whole life. I wish that Kelty could have held on and experienced this too. But I guess everything happens for a reason. as you keep telling me!

It was a wonderful gift.

When she didn't call on the scheduled night, I wasn't too worried. The next evening at a dinner party, my friends and I talked about Kelty. Even though it was nearly nine years since he had died, I said, I was only just beginning to feel better and to move on. They agreed that I seemed to be more myself, and we had a wonderful conversation about our lives.

When I got home at about 10, I decided to try Rye and dialled her cell phone. A man answered. When I said "Who's this?" he replied: "Who's this?"

I felt a familiar prickle of fear.

"This is Riley's mother. Where's Riley?"

His English was broken. "Riley's dead. Riley's dead."

I couldn't believe what I was hearing. "What do you mean, Riley's dead?"

He just kept repeating it. "Riley's dead. I'm Thai police. Riley's dead. When are you coming for the body?"

The panic rose in my throat. "No, no, what are you talking about?"

Finally he said: "You call half an hour later. English-speaking man be on phone."

He hung up. For a few seconds, I sat there in our living room, paralyzed. I was home alone; Kerry was in Vancouver, heading out the next morning for his annual Winnipeg duck hunt. When I reached him, I was hysterical, in tears, and could barely get the words out. He told me to hang on, that he was coming right home.

Kerry phoned our neighbour Cheryl, who came straight over. I phoned Britt's mom, Colleen. "Colleen, Riley's dead. Riley died. I don't know what to do." Colleen came over, too. I was a complete mess, and the two of them got me into the car and drove me to the clinic. The doctors there gave me a sedative to calm me down.

I don't remember much else about that night or the days that followed. I was in a haze, the kind of numb you can't even imagine until your child dies and your body shuts down. How could this be happening again? Was it even real? What was going on? Riley had worked so hard to stay alive. She couldn't be dead. Kelty was dead. Riley couldn't be dead, too.

I think back now on how difficult it must have been for Kerry, driving alone along the highway from Vancouver to Whistler, an hour and a half in the dark, left to his own thoughts and fears. At some point that night, after Kerry got home and starting making phone calls, the Thai police confirmed the worst.

It was October 8, 2009, and the unthinkable had happened. We had lost Riley. Our children, both our babies, were gone.

The next day, still in a fog but needing to do something, I phoned our local MP, John Weston. We didn't know how to go about getting Riley's body back to Canada, and we needed someone to deal with the Thai officials on our behalf. John was so helpful, calling Ottawa and urging the Canadian representatives on the ground in Thailand to get us some answers. I also phoned one of my long-time IBM customers, John Dominelli, someone I had been close to and trusted. John hired a private investigator, because the Thai police weren't forthcoming with the details related to Riley's death. We didn't know yet how she died or when. We only knew that she had been found in her hotel room by the housekeeper.

I couldn't get the thought out of my head that Riley, my sweet girl who could never bear to be alone, had died alone. It tore my heart apart. How could I have let that happen? It was my fault that she was dead.

At first, Kerry and I planned to go to Thailand to bring Riley's body back home. Wouldn't we be abandoning her otherwise? But the truth was that I could barely get out of bed. Kerry was my pillar of strength, and he gently convinced me that we should both stay home and let the authorities do their job on our behalf. Riley was safe now and would be home soon.

Once the Canadian consulate got involved, an autopsy was performed and we learned that Riley had not been drinking or taking drugs before she died. What she hadn't told me during our many calls, though, was that she had re-separated her shoulder while she was in Chiang Mai. A doctor had given her some medication. It turned out it was far too strong for her, and she had died of a heart attack. She had gone to sleep and never woken up.

I found some solace in that. Riley hadn't been in pain. She was feeling good about herself and looking forward to the future. Riley had certainly had her struggles throughout her teens and young adulthood, but unlike her boisterous, share-it-all brother, she had kept much of that inner tur-moil to herself. Because she couldn't control the loss of her brother, or the loss of her "complete" family, she began to control what she could. That's what led to her eating dis-order. Once she had conquered that, she turned to other means of taking away her pain, like drinking. We were blessed that, in both cases, our daughter had recognized that she needed rescuing, and she had trusted us enough to ask for help in conquering those emotional and physical demons.

In her own way, Riley had chosen hope. In the pursuit of yoga and the practice of Buddhism, she had found peace, purpose, and a healthy lifestyle that once again made her feel safe and complete. She had blossomed into a contented soul with a bright future, as beautiful on the inside as she was on the outside. I had to believe that she had fallen asleep a happy young woman and was now in a better place with her beloved brother.

The funeral was held on October 21 at Our Lady of the Mountains Catholic Church, the same church where we had said goodbye to Kelty. A number of people spoke, including Riley's cousins Tegan and Katie. "I know you felt like you were always searching, Ri; you always thought that everyone else had it more together than you," Tegan read to the congregation. "The truth is that you were way more together than any of us were and possibly ever will be."

Britt read a poem she had written. It was hard to watch her struggle through the words, but I knew Rye would have been proud of her strength. Britt was in Los Angeles when her mother called to tell her her best friend had died, and she told us later that she knew the moment she heard her mother's voice. Her poem, "For Riley Rae," was an intimate ode to their friendship, tender and mature.

I hadn't spoken at Kelty's service, but I wanted to say something at Riley's. I don't know how I managed to keep my composure, and I barely did. Nonetheless, standing up before everyone to open my heart about the loss of my daughter somehow seemed to be part of the healing I needed. I read out a letter I had written to Riley. I wanted to share with everyone her gentle spirit, her will to live from the time she was a baby, her love of sports. I needed to say out loud that although our loss was unbearable, our time with Riley was a precious memory, and there was much to celebrate.

I talked about how Riley had loved clothes, and not just any clothes but the best and the priciest. Everyone smiled when I recalled the time she came home with a lovely green sweater and proudly announced she had bought it at Value Village, which prompted me to say, "There is a God." Words could not describe the emptiness in our hearts, I said, knowing we would never see her beautiful smile again. "I will miss you beyond belief and will try not to think about all the things that could have been. Rye, go in peace, my sweet beautiful one. We will always be here for you."

My brother Ted, as he had done for Kelty, wrote a song called "Riley's Gift." He sang it accompanied by his daughter Lauren, who played the guitar I had bought for Riley when she briefly decided she was going to be a guitar player. Theirs was an achingly insightful tribute that included the lyrics "In a coffee shop in Thailand, she finally got the news / The person she was looking for was standing in her shoes." Riley's favourite music rang throughout the church, meaningful songs like Sarah McLachlan's "I Will Remember You" and Van Morrison's "Sweet Thing."

The theme of the reception was Riley's recent embracing of Buddhism, and it seemed so fitting. Every person who came put a pebble into a bowl of water. Today those pebbles sit in a bowl on the coffee table in the great room of our house, a quiet reminder of the peace our daughter had found.

One afternoon in the days that followed, when Britt was visiting us with her parents, she said out of the blue, "Ginny, do you mind if I go down to Riley's room?"

Riley had always kept journals, and Britt wanted to read some of them. I had seen the journals in Riley's room but of course had never read them myself. Britt came up a little while later. "Ginny, I think there's something in Riley's journal that you need to hear."

It was a passage from a few years previously, in which Riley was writing about a visit in Winnipeg with her grandmother, Dodie: "Oh boy, here's Dodo. She can't remember this and she can't remember that. I don't think getting old is all that it's cracked up to be. I don't think I'm going to be an old person. For what I've been through in my life, I don't think I'm going to be old. But that's okay. I have lived a really good life and I accept that I might not grow to be an old person."

It was as if she had known. I let Britt take the journals, and I'm glad she has them. They are an intimate piece of Riley that is best protected by her best friend. After Kelty's death, the journal he had started just before he died had disappeared from his room. We had never found out where it went, but we hoped it too was in safekeeping, with someone who had been important to Kelty.

Even though we had held the funeral, Riley's body was still in Thailand, red tape holding up her return home. When she finally arrived at Vancouver airport, a week or so after the service, her body was picked up by the funeral home. I wanted to see her, but I was talked out of going to the funeral home. Keep your memories of when she was alive, everyone said. I ached to hold my daughter, to say goodbye one last time, but I was too much of a basket case to fight it. I wonder to this day if that was the right decision. I had said a proper goodbye to Kelty, had held his hand and kissed him and told him that I loved him. But I didn't get to say goodbye to Riley, to kiss her forehead and brush my hand over her sweet cheek. That haunts me still.

A few days before Riley's funeral, a letter had come in the mail. It was from the Poetry Institute of Canada, advising Riley that a poem she had written, called "Untitled," had been selected for a book the institute was publishing. A copy now sits on our great room bookshelf, the page with her entry well thumbed. Neither Kerry nor I even knew that Riley had written poetry, but the poem's maturity and insight did not surprise us. It was a reflection of all that she was, deep and thoughtful and caring. Her cousin Jesse sang the poem at Riley's service, and our tears were full of pride.

Not long afterward, Riley's yoga certificate, qualifying her as a teacher, arrived from Thailand.

(6)

······················

Life Ever After

······················

PEOPLE SAY THAT when you lose a child, you become a member of a special club, a club that no parent ever wants to be part of. It's true. There is a monumental shift at the core of your being, an internal switch that resets your life to a new normal that's anything but normal. Even as time heals and life goes on, you are no longer the same person you once were.

It's as if the universe has been turned on its head. Children are meant to outlive their parents. Parents are meant to watch their sons and daughters mature into adulthood, go to work, find a life partner and, in a perfect world, marry and have their own children. Parents are supposed to become grandparents, basking in the glow of knowing they've done their job as well as they could and have earned the right to spoil the family's next generation.

When death steals the promise of your future and destroys nature's ordained plan, there is no getting over it. Although memories and photographs provide an ethereal connection to the past, and you are thankful to have them, nothing fills the void of not being able to hug your child again. Nothing prepares you for the reality that you will never again hear the sound of your son's laughter echoing down the hallway or kiss the light sprinkling of freckles across your daughter's nose.

I will never again curl up on the couch with Riley, a bowl of popcorn balanced on our knees while we watch her favourite shows, *House* and *America's Next Top Model*. I will never again sit on the sidelines in a cold arena, my breath visible, my hands warm in woolen mittens, cheering on Kelty while he skates like a dream for whatever hockey team is lucky enough to have him. Kerry and I will never get another little note from our kids, handwritten with their distinctive flourishes, like the note Riley wrote to us when she was ten, with all its glorious misspellings. "Happy 17th Anavercery," it said on the front, and, inside: "To: Mom and Dad, Hope you have a gret anavercery and I hope you have good trip! From Riley. Roses are Red vilots are blue sugar is sweet and so are both of you."

I won't be able to laugh at Kelty's silly but amazing imitation of the William Wallace character from his favourite film, *Braveheart*. I won't be rolling my eyes as he describes the antics of goofy Adam Sandler, who never made a movie Kelty didn't love. I will never dance at my son's wedding or feel tears of joy as my daughter tries on her wedding gown for the first time. I will never hold Riley's hand and whisper encouragement in her ear as she gives birth to her own babies. I will never know what it's like to have a son-in-law or a daughter-in-law, to have the privilege of welcoming a family of in-laws to our fold. Kerry and I will never be blessed to hear a precious grandchild call us Grams or

Gramps, a child of our children, who is all sticky kisses and tiny bear hugs. We won't be turning one of the spare bedrooms in our empty nest into a nursery or a playroom so that we have a good excuse for sleepovers.

We will have none of this.

When my children died, I became a different person, and people began to look at me differently. I was a social alien of sorts, one of those poor mothers who had tragically lost a child, and then tragically lost the other. People, well meaning as they are, are afraid. They are afraid that by mentioning the loss, much less your children's names, it will make you relive everything; they are afraid to talk about their own children and grandchildren, to show photos and brag about their accomplishments; they are afraid to say the wrong thing. They worry that if they tell me about how their teenager is getting into trouble or not living up to their expectations, I might be thinking, well, at least your child is alive, and I would give anything to have my children back, even with all the hardships a parent goes through. As difficult as it's been for me to engage in some of those conversations, because I do have those thoughts, I know it's difficult for them, too, especially those closest to me.

In the first few weeks after both my children died, it was easier just to stay home, cloistered in the safety of the family net. I couldn't face the world. I didn't want to see people. I didn't want people to look at me differently.

As she had done when Kelty died, my sister Cath came to stay after we lost Riley. My best friend, Clare, who has been with me through everything since our school days in Winnipeg, came and stayed with me, too. She was such a comfort, and we would spend hours curled up on my bed talking.

I realized soon enough that even if my life had twice stood still, I needed to pull myself out of the darkness and find a way to live without Kelty and Riley. I made myself go out for the occasional coffee or drink with a girlfriend, trying to establish a new routine. I found much peace in walking alone, lost in my thoughts, along the paths and trails in the glorious Whistler wilderness.

After Kelty died, I met a wonderful woman who told me something I often think about. Stephanie had lost a daughter in an accident and a brother to suicide. Those of us who have lost a child speak a different language, she said, and I knew instantly what she meant. It is not a language you want to learn, but grieving parents understand each other.

When suicide takes your child, the bond among grieving parents is about more than the loss. It's about the stigma that exists around the topic of suicide. Despite the devastating statistics, despite its ravaging of every age group and every social strata, depression is still too often whispered about, treated more like a shameful aberration than the crippling disease it is.

Kerry and I felt we had a duty to reverse that stigma, to educate. That was one of the reasons we handed out Kelty's suicide note at his service—and one of the reasons we started the Kelty Patrick Dennehy Foundation. There is nothing to hide. The more we learned, the more puzzled we were. In an age in which communication and information are so powerful and pervasive, why aren't people talking more openly about youth and depression-related suicide, especially since suicide is the second leading cause of teenage deaths in Canada, and the incidences of both attempts and successful suicides have increased by 300 per cent in the past three decades? Why, we wondered, have less than a third of those who commit suicide been identified by medical experts as suffering from depression? Why do so few of those sufferers receive treatment, and why are there so few places for them to get information and immediate, hands-on help?

We wondered, too, why there wasn't more universal discussion on the medical front so that parents would have a better understanding of the symptoms, just as they do for measles or chicken pox. The majority of suicide victims show signs of their intentions in advance of the act, usually overtures of love for family and friends. And the sad truth is that the stigma surrounding suicide means the statistics we have may only scratch at the surface of the problem.

After Kelty's death, I know some people thought I should have done something to stop him from taking his life. It was as if I could hear them thinking, "What kind of a mother is she? How could she not have seen the signs? How could she not have saved him? That's her job."

But I knew that Kerry and I had done the best we could as parents. Once we understood that our son was suffering, we did everything within our power to help him. We did research, grilled the experts, consulted doctors and therapists, and made sure he took the prescribed medication. We talked to him and monitored him, marshalling every resource at our disposal as we desperately tried to pull our boy out of the darkness and help him to understand that depression wasn't the end. But he was too young to understand that what we were telling him was true, too young to have the strength to go on.

I have never felt angry about Kelty's death, nor have I felt guilty. I know that he was just too wrapped up in his own pain to stray from his plan. We know now he had a plan to end his life, a carefully laid plan, from the moment he convinced me to go on the business trip to Florida. He said his goodbyes to his friends, his sister, and his dad on the day he died. He planned to hang himself in my office, in our house, because that's where he felt safe. He carefully moved a favourite family photo so that he could see it before he died. And he planned his loving, poignant suicide note, telling us not to worry, that his life in heaven would be better than it was on Earth.

If I beat myself up over anything, it's wishing I had known more about depression-related suicide among teens. There were signals I didn't recognize as signals until it was too late. What would I have done differently? I would never have gone away. I don't think Kelty would have taken his life if I was at home. I think he felt I couldn't handle it, but his big strong dad could. Kerry talks about how he shouldn't have gone skiing that day, but that isn't realistic. If Kelty wanted to kill himself, he was going to kill himself. He could have thrown himself in front of a car or found another way to achieve his goal.

When Kelty died, I wanted my life to be over, too. I felt the same way when I lost Riley. I wanted to be with my children and nowhere else. I didn't feel strong enough to go on without them. Kerry understood how I was feeling, but it upset him. He was worried about me and angry that I was selfish enough to think of leaving him behind.

Some marriages fail after the loss of a son or daughter. Tragedy can lay waste to a family unit and exacerbate already unsettling issues between spouses. Too often, blame goes looking for a home. Even if there is none, the memories and the pain that come with staying together often cannot be surmounted by the parents left behind to grieve.

In her book, *The Bereaved Parent*, published in 1977, author Harriet Schiff estimates that 80 to 90 per cent of marriages end in divorce following a child's death. Recent studies put the figure closer to one in five. Many of those who divorce do so for reasons other than their loss. But no matter the numbers, the truth is that the intimacy between a husband and wife can become strained as each parent struggles to cope with the loss of their child. That Kerry and I have survived the untenable—losing both our children—is a testimony, I think, to our ability to find comfort and strength in the kind of person each of us is. We may have lost our cherished children, but we have not lost what we have long cherished in each other. In many ways, we have become stronger, both as individuals and as a couple. What gets us up in the morning is that strength and our mutual respect. We need each other more now than we ever did, and we need to preserve the memory of Kelty and Riley. With our loss has come a new closeness. Our love and our children are what bond us now.

People say things will get easier as time marches on, but they don't. The loss of Kelty and Riley is with me every single moment of every single day. No matter how distracted I get—and I work hard at being distracted—no matter how I feel, whether I'm down in the dumps or having a great time on vacation, my kids are with me. Every night before I go to sleep, I go over the next day in my mind: how I'm going to get through it, what my plan is to keep busy, how I can face another day without them. The first thing I think about when I wake up in the morning is my children, and how I'm going to honour them that day. That is what gets me out of bed. I manage because I have to. For them.

But it will never be easy.

The month after Riley died, my nephew Rory, Cath's son, married his girlfriend, Brooke, in Hawaii. Riley was supposed to be part of the ceremony, and Kerry and I decided we needed to be there. Everyone had rallied around us during a sad time, and we needed to do the same for them in this happy time. The day was clear and beautiful, and watching Rory and Brooke exchange their vows on the beach was good for my heart. The reception was lovely, but at some point, I hit a wall. Thrilled as I was for them, it was overwhelming to realize that I would never see Kelty or Riley exchange vows. Kerry and I left early.

I had been invited to give a speech at the November Crystal Ball, the B.C. Children's Hospital annual fundraiser, and whenever I needed distraction during our time in Hawaii, I returned to our hotel room and immersed myself in preparing it. Up to that point, my public speaking had always focussed on Kelty. This was the first speech that would be about losing both my children. The hospital had kindly offered me an out after Riley died, but I felt I needed to do it. Writing words that honoured both my children seemed to help.

The speech went well, but talking in public about the loss of both of my kids was rough.

Why do I share this painful story with you? Well, like my children, who had the power of giving back, I hope that by sharing what I have learned about my children it could be a gift for you... Kelty and Riley have helped me realize what is important in life. They have helped our extended family bond together even more tightly. Over the years, I have learned so many things. I have learned to be thankful for the things that you have in life and the things that you don't have or have lost. As I always said to Riley, everything happens for a reason.

To this day, every time I get up to give a speech, Kelty and Riley are right there with me. I can feel them, beautiful angels sitting on my shoulder, proud of me for doing so much for others in their name.

A month after that speech, we had to face Christmas: the first Christmas in twenty-three years without one of our children to celebrate it with. Kerry and I decided to spend the holidays with our families in Winnipeg. Kerry's mom hadn't been well, and my dad had been sick, too. We needed to see them. A few weeks before we left, Kerry and I went skating on Green Lake. He laced up his hockey skates and I dug out the old ice skates I hadn't worn for ages. We skated all the way to the end of the lake and back, the sun on our faces, the snow-draped mountains a breathtaking backdrop. After a time, I headed back to the house to do some baking. Kerry stayed behind to play a bit of hockey with the families having fun out on the ice. I was up to my elbows in flour when the phone rang. "Gin." It was Kerry. "Come and get me. And bring the car."

He had fallen and broken his hip. The same hip had been operated on years before and was held together with a metal rod. Once the clinic in Whistler determined it was broken, they referred us to Lions Gate Hospital in North Vancouver. It was late, so we went home, planning to head to Vancouver the next day. But in the morning, Kerry could barely get out of bed. It took me forty-five minutes to get him into the car, and it was only when I conscripted the help of our friend Garry that we managed at all. The Lions Gate diagnosis was simple: there was nothing they could do because of the rod. The hip would have to heal itself, and that meant that Kerry couldn't do anything except rest for a week. I trundled him back into the car with the aid of some doctors who happened to be in the parking lot, and drove him to his North Vancouver place.

By then, Kerry was working as chief executive officer for the Pacifica Treatment Centre, a job he had taken in the spring of 2009. An oasis of residential drug and alcohol treatment in the heart of east Vancouver, Pacifica offers an extensive three-level program, including out-patient counselling, and it has helped more than ten thousand people deal with their addictions since it opened in 1977. Since the job would have meant a daily commute from Whistler for Kerry, which was out of the question, he lived during the week in North Vancouver, heading home to Whistler for the weekends. Janice, the family friend he stayed with during the week, was fantastic when I delivered my hip-damaged husband to her, and she promised to keep an eye on him.

Confident that my husband was in good hands, I went to Winnipeg as scheduled. Kerry joined me there a few days before Christmas. We had a lovely dinner at Cath's, a wonderful family gathering around the dinner table. With Kerry on crutches and Dodie using a walker, it was a bit chaotic, but the distraction of helping them somehow made Christmas bearable. When we returned to Whistler before New Year's, though, the reminder that Christmas would never be the same for us was stark: the house was so big and empty. There was no tree, no stockings filled with surprises and treats, no echo of my delighted kids ripping open a gift.

Throughout it all, Kerry was wonderful. He knows me like no one else and can sense my moods, tell when I need to be alone or when encouraging words will boost my spirits. "Gin, they are no longer suffering," he would say. "They are no longer in pain. You don't have to worry about them anymore."

I try not to feel sorry for myself, but there are times when I get lost in sadness, missing Kelty and Riley so much and wanting them with me. Anniversaries, birthdays, and vacations are the worst, vivid annual reminders of what has changed. When I wake up on those days, it's good to have focus. I get up and head to my spin class, go for a walk, or spend all day working on foundation business. I have learned that you can't just stop. As much as you want to shut down when you lose a child, you can't.

As when Kelty died, we had Riley cremated. Britt took some of the ashes, and we buried the rest in an urn beside Kelty's, with simple plaques marking their resting place. I visit their graves often, and it brings me a kind of contentment. I feel they are with me there. I talk to them about everything, not just how much I love and miss them but what's going on in our lives and the lives of their friends. When spring comes and the wildflowers bloom around their graves, I am reminded of life's beauty and promise. In winter, deep, soft snow covers them like a protective blanket. Their ashes are safe in the earth, and their spirits are free.

The fall after Kelty died, the high school asked if they could plant a tree on the school grounds in his honour. Today, it has grown straight and tall, fresh and green in spring, dropping a thick layer of leaves every fall onto a rock near its trunk that's embedded with a small plaque: "In Memory, Kelty Patrick Dennehy 1983–2001." I often walk the path my children walked every day to school to visit the tree, feeling its strength as its branches spread and reach for the sun.

Kerry had a memorial bench installed on the edge of Green Lake, on the public walkway close to our back deck, the summer after we lost Kelty. The plaque reads "Our Beautiful Boy, Kelty Patrick Dennehy, Nov. 23/83–Mar. 2/01." When we lost Riley, he added "Our Sweet Babes, Riley Rae Dennehy, Jul. 3/86–Oct. 8/09." I sit on that bench on many days, taking in the thickly treed mountains, the still waters of the lake, and the scudding clouds that envelop the valleys beyond. My children, I know, are there with me. Sometimes when a stranger is sitting on our bench it unsettles me, as if there is a sacredness about it that is for the Dennehys alone.

My days are filled with a different routine now. Exercise in the morning, meeting friends for lunch or coffee and, of course, foundation business. For a time after Riley died, I pursued a diversion she had encouraged me in: selling jewellery as a home sales business. Riley always said it was the perfect side job for me, and she was right. After she was gone, it gave me a reason to get up in the morning and get myself out of the house, to be with people and talk about things other than losing my children. The jewellery parties were great fun, and I reconnected with a lot of people in the community.

The first months after Riley was gone were also made easier by the arrival in Whistler of our nephew Quinn, the son of Kerry's brother Shaun. We were happy to have him. Quinn worked on the mountain and spent his spare time snowboarding and making new friends. I would whip up batches of chocolate chip cookies for them, revelling in the spirited young people who livened up our too-quiet house.

Kerry was making noises about leaving Whistler altogether, though. He didn't like me being up there by myself while he was in Vancouver working during the week. The house was so big for just the two of us. He thought it might be best for us if we sold the house and bought a condo in Vancouver, where we could be together and away from the memories.

At first I agreed with him. Maybe it would be good to have such a radical change. But my gut was telling me the time wasn't right: if I left the house, it would be like abandoning the kids.

While we were grappling with the decision, I flew to Toronto to visit some of my old IBM friends. A group of us, all women, went up to stay in cottage country, and we were out shopping one day when I wandered into a local artist's shop. Right away, a painting caught my eye: a row of colourful beach shacks titled *Moving On*. I also noticed, on an easel, a photograph of a lovely girl the artist told me was his daughter. We had a nice conversation, but although I kept going back to the painting, I didn't buy it. Back home, I regretted that, realizing that the painting would be the perfect Christmas gift for Kerry. When I sent the artist a letter telling him our story, he shipped the painting out to me with a note saying it was his gift. His daughter had suffered from depression, he said, and our story had resonance for him.

In the end, the real estate market made the decision about the possible condo for us. It wasn't the right time to sell the Nicklaus house, so we didn't. There's no question, though, that it has been difficult to stay in the house. We had cleaned out most of Kelty's room already, and Cath and Tegan went through Riley's room right after she died, because I couldn't face it. We kept personal items from both kids—cards and artwork and toys like Riley's "Beautiful Baby" doll—that are today stored in keepsake boxes. But there are still traces of them all over the house. Once in a while, I open a drawer and I am instantly filled with sorrow, transported into the past by Riley's favourite fridge magnet or a scribble of Kelty's on a piece of paper. And yet I need reminders around me. Family photographs fill our bookcases, our life story captured in picture frames. There is a snapshot of the four of us on the Panama cruise; a photo of model-pretty Riley in a purple dress; the picture of Kerry, Riley, and me wearing yellow rain slickers on the day we buried Kelty's ashes.

Downstairs, the sports room is devoted to their memory. Hockey and golf medals and trophies line the shelves. The kids' hockey jerseys hang on the wall, and everywhere you turn there are framed accolades and peewee hockey pennants. The jersey Riley wore to play forward for the Whistler Winterhawks in the 2002 B.C. Winter Games is framed with a photo of her team. Kelty's Notre Dame hockey jersey, white with red trim, is also framed, its front covered with Sharpie inscriptions from his friends: *Pippy, you were more awesome than you knew… Thanks for making my days better at N.D… Kelty, your impact on us will be measured by the legacy you left behind… We will miss you and will learn by your passing.*

People ask me all the time how I can get up every morning and walk out of our bedroom and into that empty space that was once filled by our children. They wonder how I can still work in the loft office where Kelty hung himself. But my office is the place my son felt safe enough to take his life. It's the spot where Riley would come and keep me company, ask me to braid her hair while we talked about girl things. It's hard to explain to others, but I'm comfortable working up there on the computer. Like so many places I go now that they're gone, I feel my children with me.

As 2010 loomed, Kerry and I decided to vacate the house for friends who planned to be in town to enjoy the Olympics. At the generous offer of a friend, Andrew Prossen, we joined an expedition to the Antarctic with his tour company. Kerry and I flew to Ushuaia, Argentina, for the nineteen-day cruise. The boat was an old Russian spy ship that accommodated ninety guests. We not only met some amazing people but took in tours guided by experts who knew every detail about the fascinating flora and fauna. We often shared dinner and drinks with a couple from Australia, and one night I told them about losing Kelty and Riley. Kerry said later he thought it was something I should keep to myself. But that's who I am. I wasn't shouting it to the skies, but I couldn't hear other people talk about their children without mentioning my own. When people ask me today if I have children, I always say, "Yes, I have two children. And I lost them both."

After the cruise, we stayed on for a few days in Argentina, holing up in a little rental while exploring the culture. We made it home for the Paralympics in early March. My sister Nancy, who was volunteering at the games, was staying with us, which helped with the transition back to the house. Sadly, shortly after our return, our little dog, Kelly, died. She had been so much a part of our lives, and so loved by Kelty and Riley, that it was like losing a little part of them.

Kerry and I went back to Winnipeg that summer, the first time we'd taken our annual vacation without one or both of the children. It was tough seeing people we hadn't seen since Riley died. Some didn't know what to say, and with them, our loss was like the proverbial elephant in the room. But I always tried to make people comfortable enough to have the conversation. If we didn't bring Riley up, it was as if she hadn't existed. "Please don't be afraid to talk to me about her," I would say gently.

Life without our children is a learning curve with no end. The hardest lesson is the one that demands we move forward, because to let go of the past means letting go of Kelty and Riley, and I will never do that. Kerry has marked their memory by getting matching Gaelic tattoos of their initials, one on each arm. For me, talking about them is one way to keep Kelty and Riley alive. We are blessed that our children's friends have remained in touch with us. We try to see them as much as possible, to catch up on their lives and see where they are heading as they mature. Pat and Noah had tattoos in Kelty's honour done on their arms, each saying "KPD, The Fighting Irishman." Britt memorialized Riley with another tattoo, an Edgar Allan Poe quote: "All that we see or seem is but a dream within a dream." Underneath, it reads "Riley Rae," with the dates of Riley's birth and death.

I dream about Kelty and Riley all the time. The dreams are sometimes sad and sometimes not. Sometimes they are still babies, and sometimes it's as if I just saw them yesterday. But then I wake up and it hits me. My children are gone.

People ask me if I still talk to Kelty and Riley. Of course I do. I know that when I die we will be reunited, and I find comfort in that. Sometimes, it's the only thing that gets me through the day. People ask me, too, if I ever think about how my children might have turned out.

I have no doubt that, with time, both of them would have found health and happiness. Kelty would have gone to university because that was his plan, and he would probably have become a lawyer. His social grace, charm, and sharp mind would have brought him much success, of that I'm sure. He would be married and a father. He used to tease me that he wanted two children and that I would be called Grams. Riley, I think, would have married someone like her dad, full of life but quietly strong, a spiritual man. She wanted to be a mom but had thought she might adopt, she once told me, because there were so many kids who needed homes. There's no question she would have opened that yoga studio in Whistler, teaching new generations about the benefits of the ancient practice that had brought so much serenity into her life.

As 2011 began, life for Kerry and me settled into a new routine: me in Whistler during the week, driving back and forth to Vancouver on foundation business and for other appointments, and Kerry coming up for weekends. We went back to the things we had loved doing, with each other and with the kids. We walked and hiked and skied as often as we could. Kerry buried himself in his work. He found it rewarding to oversee the good work being done at Pacifica. That he would end up running such a place seemed fitting. The insights both of us had gained about addiction and mental health issues were a saving grace for us both.

And we refocussed on the Kelty Patrick Dennehy Foundation.

(7)

· · · · · · · · · · · · · · · · ·

Choosing Hope

· · · · · · · · · · · · · · · · ·

KERRY AND I weren't sure at first what to do with the foundation after Riley died. It had been humming along since that day in the hospital when Kelty lay dying, and in the eight years since we had raised more than $4 million. We were proud to have been part of the first-class new mental health centre at B.C. Children's Hospital. But now it was as if the wind had gone out of our sails. We wondered if it was time to take a step back.

"Gin, we've raised a lot of money," Kerry said. "We've made a difference. Now maybe we need to let the foundation carry on by itself."

I thought he might be right. But then, on October 10, 2010, Kerry and I attended the dedication of the B.C. Children's Kelty Mental Health Resource Centre, named in our son's honour. It had been made possible with an additional $450,000 grant from the foundation. In addition to speeches by dignitaries and hospital officials, we listened to the emotional testimonies of people for whom the centre represented help they desperately needed. With tears in our eyes, without needing to say it to each other, Kerry and I knew. We couldn't stop. This was just the beginning.

The Kelty Mental Health Resource Centre offers tools for health professionals, parents, and youth in several languages. Parent and youth peer support workers are available for consultation, along with information on addiction and mental health issues, options for treatment, tips for self-help and prevention, and free educational events. The centre's website, packed with information about depression and updated around the clock with news and events, features heartfelt testimonials from youth, message boards, and Q&As. Private appointments can be made, and in what is best described as a telepsychiatry service, the centre also runs a communications system that can link mental health professionals by video anywhere in British Columbia. The centre's in-house staff are knowledgeable and its resources first rate. The Kelty Mental Health Resource Centre is everything the foundation could have hoped for and more.

Once Kerry and I had decided to continue our work with the foundation, we threw ourselves into it wholeheartedly. I became president, taking over most of the duties Kerry had shouldered and drawing a nominal salary. In September 2011, the foundation entered a team of thirty riders in the GranFondo, a charity bicycle race from Vancouver to Whistler. Our goal was to cover our costs, but we ended up raising an astonishing $43,000. Sponsors like Hyundai and the Whistler Question newspaper helped up the ante, and the Ride Fore Life became our new annual event.

Teenagers today, raised on social media, are conditioned to expect answers at their fingertips, and the foundation wants to be there with the information when someone hits the keyboard. The website we've established features the stories of Kelty and Riley and a wide variety of resources, including links to articles, books, support groups, and mental health organizations specializing in the treatment of depression. One link connects people to a hotline to instant help for those who need it, be they family members or adolescents in trouble. Along with statistics on depression, the website details warning signs, a critical piece of treating the disease and preventing suicide. If the information allows even one parent or friend to recognize that a loved one is depressed, we can save lives.

We've also set up Twitter and Facebook accounts to keep the conversation going about the issues and the work that the foundation is doing. Sometimes I log on to post inspirational quotations and links I think are important. Our tracking research indicates that the foundation's website is attracting users from around the world, a sign that the need is out there. As we head into the future, the board is looking at new marketing plans to extend our online reach.

In the beginning, we had hoped the foundation would eventually become a national organization, but we soon realized we had enough to keep us busy in our own backyard. The statistics are horrifying. Teen suicide is considered the second leading cause of death for teens in Canada, and, in some years, the B.C. coroners' office has reported that suicide is the number one leading cause of teen mortality in the province. Over the years, we have given grants to the Crisis Intervention and Suicide Prevention Centre of B.C., Whistler Community Services, and depression-screening programs in schools.

As the Kelty Patrick Dennehy Foundation has evolved over the years, so, too, has the board. Some of the early enthusiasts, having done so much to get things off the ground, have moved on. Today, a new generation of members is hard at work taking us into the future. As president, I spend much of my time meeting with organizational boards and health experts, giving speeches, and attending events. My message is always the same: Depression is a disease that strikes without regard for its victim, a disease that can be treated and prevented and, most of all, a disease that needs to be talked about openly, with understanding. I deliver the message through the stories of my children, telling audiences how Kelty and Riley enriched my world through their lives and how they have defined it in death. I still get emotional, but I know this opportunity to help others is the gift my children have given me.

I am happy to say that in the eleven years since we started the foundation, there has been a sea change on the subject of depression-related suicide. There is less stigma now, and the level of awareness has been raised. People talk openly about mental health, and it has been especially heartening to watch big companies step up to the plate. The Canada Post Foundation for Mental Health not only issued special stamps—one with a life-affirming tree design—but in 2011 granted more than $2 million to forty-seven non-profit mental health groups, part of the $4.6 million it has awarded since 2008. Bell Canada launched a high-profile, multi-year charitable program in 2010 to raise funds for the treatment of mental illness and promote research and access to care across the country. Bell's 2012 campaign, Let's Talk, featured six-time Olympian Clara Hughes as national spokesperson. Hughes told Canadians about her own battles with depression, quick to stress that she is no different, despite her accomplishments, from the one in five

Canadians who will experience some form of mental illness during their lifetimes. When suicide cut short the lives of NHL stars Rick Rypien and Wade Belak in 2011, the once-quiet struggles of the tough-guy hockey enforcers became front-page news and the subject of radio talk shows. A 2012 documentary titled *Darkness and Hope: Depression, Sports and Me*, sponsored by Bell, featured Toronto sportscaster Michael Landsberg sharing his experiences.

The media and big corporations are finally getting it: mental health affects us all, not just on a personal level but on a social and economic one. To combat depression and other mental illnesses, we need to start talking about them openly, respecting them as diseases that require collective action.

Although things are better from a big-picture perspective, there is still a lingering stigma when it comes to families. People don't want to admit that their son, daughter, mom, or dad is depressed or might be suicidal. Whenever I give a speech, people come up afterward to ask for guidance. My home phone is constantly ringing, with desperate people on the other end of the line. What do I do? they ask. Where do I go? How can I get help for my child? There is still a feeling that when you or someone you love is suffering from depression, the world is a lonely place. But it's not: there are millions of people going through the same thing. Thankfully, there are more and more places to turn for information and treatment. Many of us are working to get the issue into public school classrooms, much like the current programs designed to teach youth about bullying.

In the fall of 2011, I spoke at a private function held to raise funds for a proposed Lions Gate Hospital mental health building, a facility similar to that at B.C. Children's

Hospital. The foundation had committed $100,000 to the Lions Gate initiative, and I was happy to help in any way I could. The guest of honour was Margaret Trudeau, whose keynote address focussed on her own high-profile mental health issues. I was delighted when she gave everyone a copy of her memoir, Changing My Mind, inscribing mine with "Happy Birthday—I will take your lead, Ginny." (The event had been even more special when I learned that Margaret and I share the same birthday: September 10.) Her brave decision to go public with her battles with manic depression and bipolar disorder serves notice that these diseases cut across all social lines.

Early in 2012, I accepted an invitation to speak at a future date at Notre Dame College, Kelty and Riley's school in Saskatchewan. After Kelty's death, Kerry and I had sponsored an annual scholarship in his name, and I had been thinking it might be time to fund a mental health counselling program on the campus. Like all schools, Notre Dame has had its share of students grappling with mental health issues, and there could be no more appropriate place to carry on Kelty's legacy.

After Riley's death, we thought long and hard about what to do with the foundation. We knew we had to carry on because of the difference the foundation was making. But Riley's death made us realize that the focus of the foundation needed to shift. It wasn't just about those who suffered directly from depression; it was about the people around them, the parents, siblings, friends, and family members who are also deeply affected by the disease of mental illness. Riley hadn't been depressed, but her struggles after Kelty died had been directly related to losing her brother and to having watched him grapple with the demon that is depression.

That our daughter's death was so unexpected and so unnecessary, that it happened just when her future seemed so bright, made our commitment to the Kelty Patrick Dennehy foundation that much stronger. Depression is a family affair, and Kerry and I became dedicated to honouring and creating a legacy for both our children. Among our new initiatives was the Breathe Fore Life scholarship that we started in Riley's name. And in the fall of 2012, the Jog4Joy was dedicated in Riley's honour. The five-kilometre walk/run through the streets of Vancouver to raise money and awareness for mental and emotional wellness is just one of the ways we will continue to use the foundation, and the memory of our wonderful children, to improve the lives of others.

In the spring of 2013, the Dennehys embarked on a cross-Canada bicycle ride called Journey for Life that focussed on an "ENOUGH IS ENOUGH" making-a-difference campaign for mental health.

Kerry has devoted himself to preserving the work of the foundation, and thus the memory of our children, filling a fat binder with newspaper clippings, photographs, invitations, letters from donors and medical officials, and all manner of paraphernalia. There are pamphlets and ticket stubs from our events over the years, including a silver invitation inscribed with white orchids for the November 27, 2008, Crystal Ball at the Four Seasons Hotel in Vancouver. A 2011 newspaper clipping, topped by a beaming photograph of Riley, describes the Riley Dennehy Breathe Fore Life Yoga Teaching Training Scholarship Program, which Kerry and I set up through the Whistler Yoga Conference to commemorate her. The $1,000 grant is intended for up-and-coming yoga enthusiasts who want to pursue their spiritual and physical passion, just as Riley had done.

And there are letters of gratitude in the binder, too, some of them hard to read. One, dated June 2007, and forwarded to us by the British Columbia Transplant Society, is an unsigned card from the man who received Kelty's liver. The recipient, a father of five and grandfather to six, wrote the message while on a ferry on his way to his sixth annual checkup. "I thank you for this wonderful gift," he said. "May you forever be blessed."

This is our work now, through the foundation and its outreach: to tell our family's story, to increase awareness about depression, and to provide resources to help all those others struggling with the soul-destroying disorders that rip families apart. Our dream is that one day there will be a Kelty Mental Health Resource Centre in every major hospital across Canada and education programs in every public school in the country. We dream that depression will one day be a stigma-free disease like cancer, with the same kind of widespread awareness and funding. Our job is also to teach others that even in the face of the unthinkable, you can choose hope. That is now our way of life. We have chosen hope for others, and in doing so we are creating an ongoing legacy that means our children will never be forgotten.

People say to me, "Ginny, how do you do it? How do you keep going?" And I think, "I'm not that special. I do it because I have to." I have chosen to live a healthy life so that I can honour my children, carry on this work on their behalf. I'm lucky; I have not only a big, close-knit family but also wonderful friends. I couldn't do this without the LOLs, the Ladies of Leisure, a group of ten women who have been gathering once a year for decades, weathering personal storms together and supporting each other through marriage and divorce, birth and death. I belong to a book club and have another group of zany friends who put on the annual Non-Perspiring Olympics, which involves all sorts of crazy activities, such as three-legged races and scavenger hunts. There are friends from IBM and from Whistler, Winnipeg, Toronto, and Vancouver. I have relied upon each one of them. Through many a tear, they have helped me find laughter. Every single day they bring me inspiration and the will to get up and get on with things.

I get so much inspiration from Kerry. I know one day we'll turn the foundation over to others to carry on our children's legacy and spend more time together, more time skiing through fresh powder on the mountain, more time travelling and relaxing in the dry desert air, which is Kerry's dream.

And, of course, I get inspiration from my children.

To lose one child seems inconceivable. To lose two is not only rare, it seems beyond human comprehension. There is always a rawness sitting on the edge of your emotions, a searing pain. The hardest parts are the indelible images, the visions of your children that are still so clear you feel you could reach out and touch them. Your beautiful boy's sunburned face as he lay dying, your lovely daughter walking toward the airplane that would fly her out of your life forever. It has been indescribably tough for Kerry and me. Our sorrow often seems to swallow us. But life, as it must, goes on, and so must we.

I am lonely without my beautiful babies, and nothing will ever heal the hole in my heart. But I can't focus on that hole. If I do, then I'm not doing what Kelty and Riley would want me to do. That's the gift I got from both of them.

Today, my son and my daughter are together again, brother and sister, buried side by side in the small cemetery off Westside Road in Whistler, a secluded spot on top of a mountain thick with majestic trees and home to a cold, clear brook.

Their granite headstones are flat to the earth and simple.

Our Beautiful Boy
KELTY PATRICK DENNEHY
Nov 23/83 to Mar 2/01

Our Beautiful Babes
RILEY RAE DENNEHY
Jul 3/86 to Oct 8/09

Today, as I choose hope, I don't just have one angel on my shoulders giving me courage and strength.

I have two.

The Kelty Patrick Dennehy Foundation

SINCE ITS ESTABLISHMENT in 2001, the Kelty Patrick Dennehy Foundation has raised $4.3 million. In the past eleven years, our grants and commitments have included the following:

> $1 million to the B.C. Children's Hospital to create a mental health facility for youth and children specializing in treatment, education, and research
> $450,000 to create the Kelty Mental Health Resource Centre at B.C. Children's Hospital
> $500,000 to support the establishment of a chair at the UBC/VGH Centre of Excellence for Depression Research
> a $100,000 commitment to the B.C. Crisis Centre to fund the delivery of suicide prevention and stress management workshops to youth and to support www.youthinbc.com, a one-on-one chat line, and 1-800 phone lines for youth in distress
> a $100,000 commitment, as part of a $500,000 commitment, to the Lion's Gate Hospital Foundation toward a

Kelty Dennehy Resource Centre in the new Hope Centre, to be completed in the fall of 2013

In the next five years, the foundation is determined to work closely with the B.C. government to become the leading organization in British Columbia for suicide and depression prevention. The foundation will continue to support already established government institutions, such as the Lions Gate Hospital, B.C. Children's Hospital, and the B.C. Crisis Centre. The overall vision for the foundation is to establish a Kelty Mental Health Resource Centre in major hospitals where needed across Canada.

Another program in development is the building of community models for awareness and prevention to be implemented in every district across the province, with an eventual goal of going Canada-wide. These culturally inclusive community models, run at both the high-school and the elementary-school level, will increase discussion about the signs of mental illness while encouraging kids and teens to fight this together.

The foundation's fundraising initiatives will be focussed on individual donations, fundraising events, and large corporate sponsorships. The foundation is also positioning itself to receive grant funding and provincial financial support.

Getting youth involved is one of the keys to the success of the foundation. Our goals include encouraging all communities to engage young adults in a variety of annual public events that not only raise funds but also raise awareness about depression and its debilitating toll on families. Only by removing the stigma of this disease, which affects too many young people, will we win the war and end depression's indiscriminate devastation. With this book and the ongoing work of the foundation, we are reaching out to individuals and communities at every level. We need your help, and by working together at a grassroots level, we can tackle this disease in the stark light of day. A doctor at B.C. Children's Hospital told us that the early detection of mental illness could save the lives of many young people, and the foundation has vowed to try to do just that. With the support of the community, the medical establishment, and your help as individuals, we can make a difference.

Chances are depression will affect someone you love. Be it your daughter, son, niece, nephew, or a family friend, you can ensure they will have the resources to help them by donating to the Kelty Patrick Dennehy Foundation. We are a leader in the fight to save young lives, and your help will change the way mental health resources are accessed in this country.

The Kelty Patrick Dennehy Foundation:
www.thekeltyfoundation.org

The Kelty Mental Health Resource Centre,
B.C. Children's Hospital: keltymentalhealth.ca

facebook.com/keltyfoundation

twitter@kelty

Teenage Depression and Suicide: Warning Signs and How to Help

There are several behavioural indicators that can help parents or friends recognize the threat of suicide in a loved one. Since mental and substance-related disorders frequently accompany suicidal behaviour, many of the cues to be looked for are symptoms associated with such disorders as depression, bipolar disorder (manic depression), anxiety disorders, alcohol and drug use, disruptive behaviour disorders, and schizophrenia.

Some common symptoms of these disorders include:
> Extreme personality changes
> Loss of interest in activities that used to be enjoyable
> Significant loss or gain in appetite
> Difficulty falling asleep or staying asleep or wanting to sleep all day
> Fatigue or loss of energy
> Feelings of worthlessness or guilt

> Withdrawal from family and friends
> Neglect of personal appearance or hygiene
> Sadness, irritability, or indifference
> Having trouble concentrating
> Extreme anxiety or panic
> Drug or alcohol use or abuse
> Aggressive, destructive, or defiant behaviour
> Poor school performance
> Hallucinations or unusual beliefs

Tragically, many of these signs go unrecognized. Although suffering from one of these symptoms certainly does not imply that one is suicidal, it's always best to communicate openly with a loved one who is demonstrating more of these behaviours, especially if these behaviours are out of character. Here are some obvious signs to look for if someone you love is contemplating suicide.

> Putting one's affairs in order
> Giving or throwing away favourite belongings
> Talk of death or suicide

HOW TO HELP

People contemplating suicide feel so alone and helpless. The most important thing to do if you think a friend or loved one is suicidal is to communicate with them openly and frequently. Make it clear that you care and stress your willingness to listen. Be sure to take all talk of suicide seriously. Don't assume that people who talk about killing themselves will not follow through. An estimated 80 per cent of all those who commit suicide give some warning of their intentions to a friend or family member.

One of the most common misconceptions is that talking with someone who might be contemplating suicide may make the situation worse. This is not true. There is no danger of "giving someone the idea." Rather, the opposite is correct. Bringing up the question of suicide and discussing it without showing shock or disapproval is one of the most helpful things you can do. This openness shows that you are taking the individual seriously and responding to the severity of their distress.

Never assume that those contemplating suicide are unwilling to seek help. Studies of suicide victims show that more than half had sought medical help within six months before their deaths. It is also important that you don't leave the suicidal person to find help alone. Never assume that someone who is determined to end his or her life can't be stopped. Even the most severely depressed person has mixed feelings about death, wavering until the very last moment between wanting to live and wanting to die. Most suicidal people do not want death; they just want the pain to stop. The impulse to end it all, though, no matter how overpowering, does not last forever. The majority of young people who hear a suicide threat from a friend or loved one don't report the threat to an adult. Take all threats seriously and remember you are not betraying someone's trust by trying to keep them alive.

If you know of a friend or loved one who is contemplating suicide, it is essential to help him or her find immediate professional care. In Canada, call your provincial crisis centre or the national suicide hotline at 1-800-SUICIDE, which will provide immediate guidance and connect you to crisis centres and resources in your province. The national Kids Help Phone, 1-800-668-6868, also provides counselling and resources for those in need under the age of twenty. In the United States, call the NAMI HelpLine at 1-800-950-NAMI (6264) for more information and to help you locate your local NAMI for area assistance. If you think the threat is immediate, call 911.

Acknowledgements

TO MY AMAZING family and friends, who have always been there for me, who supported me and encouraged me even when I didn't think I could go on.

To my loving husband, Kerry, the pillar of my strength, who has never left my side on this journey but has always allowed me to take my own path on the road to healing.

A special thanks to the Kelty Patrick Dennehy Foundation and its board and to all of our donors and supporters, including our honoured Kelty Circle members and the many participants in the Ride Fore Life, Run Fore Life, Dance Fore Life, Drive Fore Life, and Breathe Fore Life fundraising events. Your continuing dedication and generosity have helped us get to where we are today and will ensure that we get to where we need to go tomorrow.